STERLING & POPE
PUBLISHING CORP.
NEW YORK • DALLAS • LONDON

What readers have said about
Selling From The Heart
by Steven Lloyd

"*This is a wonderful book on selling, destined to be a classic!* Selling From The Heart is full of practical, proven techniques and methods that you can use to dramatically increase your sales. It is also easy and fun to read."

> **Brian Tracy, CPAE**
> Author, Psychology of Selling
> Chairman of the Board
> BRIAN TRACY INTERNATIONAL

"*A masterpiece!* I have been teaching professional salesmanship for 32 years and this is the most powerful, practical, and results oriented book I have ever read! This well written treasure is truly a skill based system that will bring major rewards to anyone that will invest its wisdom in themselves and their future. Congratulations on redefining the word, *classic!*"

> **Joe Charbonneau, CSP, CPAE**
> Professional Speaker & Trainer

"*Grand slam home run!* I have been investing in sales and management books for over half of my life. This book will travel with me personally for years to come. If every person in sales will follow your principles and systems, they will cut their success learning curve in half! Thank you for writing this *incredible book!*"

> **G. Douglas Elliott, CRS**
> Chairman of the Board
> MARKET IT, INC.

"*I couldn't put it down!* Every thought is so well written. Every idea is so valuable. What is even equally amazing is that everything taught in this book really works. *It has already improved my life and career in less than 30 days!*"

> **Michael Disney, CEO**
> DISNEY FINANCIAL

"Selling From The Heart, springs from Steven Lloyd's skill, intellect, and love for selling. Steven presents profound sales wisdom in a practical, 'How To' format that is easy and fun to read. *The lessons he will teach you in this book can be used the same day the book is read!* This book contains great exercises and examples that will lead you step by step above and beyond selling success. Steven's ideas and techniques are tried, tested, and proven systems that will improve your life and career for years to come! Steven Lloyd is a true star that has a wonderful ability to put himself into the mind of his reader and lead you into experiencing what he practices. *This is a great book!*"

Robert Henry, CSP, CPAE
President
NATIONAL SPEAKERS ASSOCIATION
1983-1984
Winner, The Cavett Award
For Speaking Excellence, 1988

"Steven Lloyd has written a book that should be required reading by anyone who wants to succeed in business, relationships, selling or, life! *If you want to do more, be more and have more...read this book!*"

Willie Jolley
International speaker
Author of
"It Only Takes A Minute To Change Your Life"
And, "A Setback Is A Setup For A Comeback!"

"*This book actually teaches you the secret to sales success!* All people buy on emotion and justify their decision with logic. Steven unlocks the mysteries of buyer motivation in an easy to learn format that obviously comes from the heart of someone who has been teaching the subject for years."

Ray Leone
International Speaker
Author of,
Success Secrets Of The Sales Funnel

Also by Steven Lloyd
For release in 2001

Success From The Heart^{SM}
Effortless Motivation^{SM}

SELLING

FROM THE HEART ®

"In The New Millennium, Selling Is Everyone's Job!"

How to master the emotional sale and take
immediate control of your personal,
professional, and economic lives!

Steven Lloyd

STERLING & POPE
PUBLISHING CORP.

NEW YORK • DALLAS • LONDON

STERLING & POPE PUBLISHING
1369 Madison Ave, PMB 432
New York, New York 10128-0711

Cover design Sterling & Pope
Artwork by Ron Wilson Illustrious
Photography by Blauvelt Master of Photography
Book layout by BookSetters
Additional editing by Jim Ottaway
Manufactured in the U.S.A.
First Printing, May 2000
Second Printing, December 2000

0 7 2 0 0 0

Library of Congress Cataloging in Publication Data

Lloyd, Steven.
  Selling from the heart : how to master the emotional sale and take immediate
control of your personal, professional, and economic lives! / Steven Lloyd.
—New York : Sterling & Pope Publishing, c2000.
    p.   cm.
"In the new millennium, selling is everyone's job!"
ISBN 0-9678616-0-8
1.   Selling. 2. Success in business. I. Title

HF5438.25 .L56   000   00-100493
658.85—dc21   CIP

Trademark, Service Mark, and Copyright Acknowledgments

Selling From The Heart^{SM}	PDR^{SM}
Managing From The Heart^{SM}	Brain Language^{SM}
Success From The Heart^{SM}	Getting Hired Vs Closing The Sale^{SM}
LocoMotivation^{SM}	Bullseye Thinking^{SM}
Image Transfer System^{SM}	Belief Replacement Training^{SM}
ITSN^{SM}	Belief Release Training^{SM}
Positronic Mind Affirmation^{SM}	BRT^{SM}
Career Resume Book^{SM}	Belief Replacement Coach^{SM}
Emotional Buying Center^{SM}	BRC^{SM}
EBC^{SM}	Negitroid^{SM}
Emotional Buying Motivation^{SM}	Nutrobot^{SM}
EBM^{SM}	Positronic^{SM}
Voice Mail Magic^{SM}	10/30-Power Formula^{SM}
Practice, Drill, and Rehearse^{SM}	Email Magic^{SM}

We believe the following words, companies, and initials to be owned by other companies and individuals and believe them to be protected by the United States Trademark Act Section 6, 15 U.S.D. Section 1056; TMEP sections 1213 and 1213.02(a). Protection may or may not be afforded under International Class 35 and International Class 41 for each of the following:

Federal Express ®
FedEx®
FedEx Express Saver ®

Hewlett Packard ®
Office Jet ®

Kinko's ®

Dunn & Bradstreet ®

Realtors ®

Radio Shack ®

The Weed Burner ®

Lazy Boy ®

Tonka ®

Microsoft ®
Windows98 ®
Dos ®

Jet Ranger ®

Rolodex ®

Hammermill ®
Jet Print Ultra ®
Ultra ®

America Online ®

Paper Direct ®

Flair ®

Sanford ®
Uni-ball ®
Micro Rollerball ®

ACKNOWLEDGMENTS

As I write these words, I feel tears welling up in my eyes, and my throat is getting thick. I have so many people to thank and I am concerned that I will forget someone and hurt their feelings.

First and foremost in my life is God. Anything that you read in this book that you see as profound comes from God. I am a mere tool, an instrument, a servant.

Next is my wife, Sherri. Thank you for loving and supporting me in ways that only those who experience being with their perfect soul mate would understand. Thank you for traveling with me for tens of thousands of miles and helping me in the many ways I have needed, without ever complaining. Thanks for your courage to grow and for believing in me. Thank you for being a terrific mom to our three kids. With every day that goes by they know you and I both love them. Most importantly, they know that we love each other. Our love and relationship stand as a shining example of what is possible. Hopefully, they will never settle for anything less. Thank you for providing a balance in our lives that is irreplaceable.

To my three wonderful children, Jim, Jessica, and Christopher-thank you for living the lives I show people that they can live. You have always made me proud of you. I am the luckiest dad in the world to have children just like you. The greatest gift we have given each other is to become adult friends. That is also the toughest bridge that parents and children will ever cross. Thank you for making this journey with me. Thanks also for allowing me to be human as well as to be your dad and now your friend.

Specials thanks to G. Douglas Elliott for your never wavering friendship and for more than 20 years of encouragement, love, and support. Words cannot describe our friendship. If everyone had just one friend like you, they would be truly wealthy!

Special thanks to Jim Turrell for being my friend and encouraging me to teach my very first "Selling From The Heart" workshop in February of 1992.

Special thanks to Dave Stone for your encouragement and investment in my speaking, training, and consulting education. I, along with the thousands of lives you touched, will miss you for all time.

Specials thanks to Roger Wakefield for giving a 19-year-old kid a chance. Thank you for requiring me to learn the basic presentation and sales closes. This training has been the foundation on which I have built my entire life and career.

To JoAnne Williams, thanks for having the vision to see the value of my work and the courage and insight to hire me to train your salespeople long before emotional based training was even acceptable.

Thank you to all those who helped me prepare and edit this work. Special thanks to Bill East for all your help, love, and support. Your encouragement and personal growth during this project was nothing less than inspiring. Your gentle style of convincing me about your edits has been truly World-Class!

Thanks to all the managers, leaders, and friends who trusted me enough to take a chance on something new.

Thanks to all the teachers and mentors who had the courage to do their work. You not only taught me, you inspired me to do mine!

To my students who have had the courage to study, learn, apply, and benefit from a new and better way of selling, "Selling From The Heart", thank you for your continued love and support. Not a day goes by that I am not thrilled when someone calls my offices to say, "I'm calling because one of your students said I really need to take your course!" You are helping me fulfill my Mission: "*To improve the way selling is done, one person at a time, From The Heart!*"

And finally, thanks to **you** for buying my book and for reading, studying, learning, and applying what I teach. From this day forward you can experience the most powerful, most wonderful way to live, work, and sell, **From Your Heart!**

Contents

FOREWORD

It was the summer of 1979 when I first met Steven Lloyd. Dave Stone, the author, speaker, international trainer, and a longtime friend of mine asked me to meet him so he could introduce me to a special young man that he had just made Vice President of the Stone Institute.

We met at the Camelot Club in Minneapolis, near my office. As soon as Mr. Stone introduced me to Steven Lloyd, Steven and I became friends and we have remained friends for over 20 years. Steven is one of those rare people that come along only a few times in your life that bless and help improve your life from the day you meet. He possesses a special kind of charisma that draws the best out of you.

Steven has the unique ability to listen closely to what you have to say and then help you to clearly define your highest potential. He also cares enough and has the courage to hold you accountable to working toward and achieving your best with a gentle but firm style, never allowing you to hide, not even from yourself. He has the biggest and most powerful heart of anyone I have ever known.

Steven Lloyd has developed his communication abilities and skills to a level presented by only a few people that I have seen in my almost 35 years of international business travel. His talent to mix passion, wisdom, humor, and results-generating skills with his speaking and training is equaled only by his writing skills. You will soon see what I mean as you read the wonderful book you are now holding in your hands.

This book will become like a cherished friend to you. Steven will teach, encourage, entertain, enlighten, and coach you step by step through the success systems that he has invested his life in developing.

As you gaze through the paper and the ink of this book, you will see him sitting with you. You will feel his heart and hear his wisdom, just as if he were in the same room with you.

I have personally witnessed and experienced both the power and the simplicity of each of the success systems he will help you to understand, as he leads you step by step through the wonderful chapters of this book.

If you will set aside what you think you know about selling and managing and embrace what you are about to be taught in this, soon to be classic work, you will be very glad you did! For over 20 years I have experienced, admired, and enjoyed watching Steven Lloyd provide individuals and organizations the opportunity to become the leaders of their industry in a very short period of time. I have seen many grow to the top of their fields almost overnight. You too will experience this same magic as you study, learn, and apply what you are about to read.

One of the greatest gifts you could give someone you truly care about is a copy of this book. One of the greatest gifts you will ever give to yourself is to read it!

> G. Douglas Elliott
> Chairman of the Board
> Market It, Inc.

INTRODUCTION

Why this book has been written is as equally important as what this book has to teach you. The sun has just set on my 29th year in professional sales and sales management. My soul cries out to give something of real and lasting value back to a profession that has given me so much. I have learned from the best of the best in these fields. You will recognize several of their names in both the acknowledgements and endorsements of this book.

This book is, to my knowledge, the first and only book to date on emotional selling. I am sure that you have heard; "All sales are made on emotion and justified with logic." As true as I believe this fact is, I have been amazed at how little information and training has been available, until now, on emotional selling, which is the CAUSE of the sale. Our emotions are rooted in our belief system. Your beliefs, and the beliefs of those that you are trying to build relationships with, are the CAUSE of your success or failure. To emphasize the importance of this fact to you, I have bolded certain words to help you to focus on them and their importance. I have used bold and small capital letters to also focus your attention on important concept words so that you can easily see these words and receive their message.

When I started in selling, I was fortunate to start my 29-year successful sales and management career under the leadership of Roger Wakefield. He was a leader who BELIEVED in and taught scripted sales presentations and **success systems**. I knew nothing! I was in real economic and emotional NEED of success. Fortunately, I was young enough (age 19) and naive enough to do exactly what I was taught to do without resisting or questioning what I was being taught. I did not deviate from his success system by even one word!

This beginning taught me a wealth of knowledge about how to design **success systems** for the companies that I would one day own. Over the past 29 years I have met many wonderful and well deserving salespeople that need what I am now ready to share. I have invested years in teaching and perfecting these **success systems**. Each of the ideas, strategies, techniques, and **success systems** contained in this book have all been thoroughly tested and proven successful in the arena of the live selling scenario.

My style is one of true "How To." My goal was to write a "Selling Cook Book." I trust that you will find each part of this book easy to read, study, and learn, and with practice even easier to demonstrate the successful results for yourself. Much like working in the kitchen of a master chef, you may not be able to produce World-Class results with your very first try but you will have good enough results to get excited enough to continue practicing!

The principles in this book will serve the full range of sales producers and managers. The systems in this book are universal and designed to serve anyone and everyone that wants to improve their communication and people skills. If you keep reading and studying this book, it will continue to reveal new and exciting ideas, strategies, techniques, **success systems**, and lessons you did not see in your first few readings. This book contains the best of what I have invested 29 years of my life learning, perfecting, and teaching.

My wish, hope, and prayer is that you use this material for good. If you do, it will benefit and bless your life as it has blessed mine as well as many others.

Please write me and let me know how these sales secrets and **success systems** have worked for you.

"**S**elling from your mind will make you a living. Selling from your Heart will make you a legend!"

—Steven Lloyd

CHAPTER ONE
What Is Selling Anyway?

THE DIFFERENCE BETWEEN MARKETING AND SELLING

All of us are trying to transfer our thoughts, feelings, and ideas to someone else. We want and need for them to like us, BELIEVE us, and trust us. Being liked, BELIEVED, and trusted are the three critical steps to "making a sale." Don't we all want other people to like us? Don't we all want other people to BELIEVE us? Don't we all want other people to trust us? The answer to all three of these questions, at least based on the thousands of people that I've interviewed, is yes! The fact is, we all sell!

It really doesn't matter what you think your job description is. Here is a Steven Lloyd-ism that will really benefit you by teaching you the truth of our new twenty-first century economy:

"In the new millennium, selling is everyone's job!"

There is an old saying, "The times they are a changing." Well, in case you have not noticed, times have already changed! The turn of the calendar from 1999 to 2000 in fact and in truth only added one more day to our lives, not another year. In application, it has served to wake us all up to the fact that we are now in a new and exciting time. This new time will require more of us all. Now that the calendar has finally flipped over to remind everyone that times have changed, you will soon see that what I am saying is true for you, too. *Selling is now everyone's job!*

For many years you have heard that it would benefit you to take a public speaking course. "Learning how to speak well in public will benefit you and your career." Sound familiar?

Millions of people have taken public speaking training. Toastmaster International's membership has boomed in the past 20 years. True to their word, corporations worldwide have promoted and compensated the people who took the speaking courses. These people's lives were improved. Well, ask yourself this question: Isn't public speaking a form of selling? Sure it is! Public speaking is just one of several sales presentation styles. When you hear a great speaker, don't you walk away from that meeting sold on something? If he or she was truly great, they sold you an idea, a concept, or a BELIEF. They sold you something!

I agree with the people who said that you should work to improve your speaking skills. Understand, however, that what they were really trying to get you to do was to learn to sell. As the worldwide economy continues to grow, it will also get more and more competitive. Only those who know how to sell will reap the really big rewards in the coming decade.

If you are a person who has any negative feelings about selling, ask yourself where those BELIEFS came from. Selling has had a bad reputation starting with the early "salespeople," called carpetbaggers. These men went from house to house selling goods following the Civil War. They preyed on the weak and beaten people who had lost most of their worldly possessions in the war. They sold them anything they could, for whatever they could get. These men were considered salespeople. I suggest to you that they were not salespeople. Salespeople are required to "move the too much," not to divide the "not enough." You don't need salespeople to sell shortages! They did not need rapport building skills and presentation techniques or relationship building skills. They were con-artists and charlatans taking advantage of desperate people. We still have people like that today. You see them show up following a natural disaster like a flood or a tornado.

They "offer" drinking water for $10 a gallon. They "sell" flashlight batteries for $5 each. These are not salespeople-they are opportunists!

A salesperson is someone who BELIEVES in what he or she is presenting, be it a product, service, or idea. How that product, service, or idea is presented is crucial to the success of the sale. There are always at least two ways of saying anything and still achieving full disclosure. If you were selling a drain cleaner that you knew was a deadly toxin and you wanted and needed to inform your prospect of its danger to his or her children, how would you present this information? Would you say, "Martha, if your children drink this product they will die?" You have accomplished full disclosure, but you have scared the customer away from wanting to own the product. Is there a more positive way of presenting the same information? What if you were to say, "Martha, the manufacturer of this amazing product has produced a drain cleaning solution that is so powerful that you must promise me to keep it under lock and key because if anyone drinks it, they will become very sick and possibly die!" Doesn't this second approach still get the warning in **and** make the sale? Isn't the second technique actually using the power of emotion to enhance the value of the product while at the same time warning the consumer of the product's potential danger? This is **Heart Selling**!

When you look at web pages on the Internet, they either sell you or they don't. Thousands of web sites are being added to the Internet every day. Even if you invest the money and hire the best web site designer that money can buy, you still have to market your site or no one will know that you even have a site. Then, your site must sell and not just present information. The more you can reach people's Hearts as well as their minds, the more successful you will become. So again, Selling From The Heart is everyone's job in the new millennium!

Heart as used in this work, is that special and sacred place within all of us where our emotions override our reason. Two Sentries protect the Heart. On the left is the **Warrior of Intellect**. On the right is the **Adviser of Emotions**.

I will guide you step-by-step-by-step past these two Guards, straight into the Heart. The success of this process has only one major requirement of you. For you to be allowed to Sell To The Heart, you first must Sell From The Heart! I will lead you step-by-step through the process of Selling To The Heart by starting with your own.

Selling From The Heart is really a process to help you learn how to master human communications. It is targeted to those who use their skills, talents, abilities, and BELIEFS to sell products or services for a living, however, it will help everyone communicate better. If you don't see yourself as a salesperson, this book will also help you prepare for the day that you realize that you already are selling. As long as you are selling anyway, wouldn't you like to get paid for it?

World-Class sales performance requires a perfect balance between sales and marketing!

Webster's dictionary defines selling as, "To exchange a product and or service for money; to offer for sale."

Webster's defines marketing as, "The process or technique of promoting an aggregate of functions involved in moving goods from producer to consumer; The trading of commerce in certain services or products."

There's a huge difference between selling and marketing. In the 29 years that I have been in professional sales, marketing, and management, I have read, listened to, or attended the vast majority of courses on selling, marketing, and management. I have invested in most of the books, listened to a large percentage of the available tapes, and yet, I have never read or heard a working definition of the **difference** between selling and marketing. Here is another Steven Lloyd-ism.

> "*The clearer your understanding is, the better your results are!*"

With clarity as my goal here, I offer you the following two definitions.

"Selling is a process and a discipline through which products and or services are delivered to a marketplace, ideally one that has been prepared to receive them."

"Marketing is a process by which a product and or service is prepared for a marketplace or a marketplace is prepared to receive them. The most EFFECTIVE marketing does both simultaneously."

If you sell professionally or manage a sales organization and you are not getting the sales performance you would like and BELIEVE you are capable of achieving, balance is where you need to start. If one side of your sales/marketing scale is not in perfect balance with the other side, your sales performance will suffer. It does not matter where you BELIEVE you are in the hierarchy of selling and marketing. If you make your living from the delivery of products or services, both are your responsibility!

The vast majority of companies that I have studied do not thoroughly understand this simple but critical difference between sales and marketing. The proof of this is evidenced in the fact that most sales/marketing companies have one senior person responsible for the results of both sales and marketing. You can easily tell which side of the scale their education comes from. Simply look at the company's sales and marketing materials and programs. If the company has great advertising, brochures, and promotional materials there is a marketing person at the helm. If the company has a multi-tiered commission and bonus plan, ongoing recruiting programs, incentive trips, and high quality training, there is a salesperson leading the sales and marketing efforts.

The best and most effective companies that I have consulted with have or are moving towards creating a balance between sales and marketing. The most effective structure that I have witnessed is to put two officers, one from each of the two disciplines, on par authority and value levels. They are also on a par reporting level to either an Executive Vice President with a general business degree, background, and or training, or reporting directly to the President of the firm. This management design creates perfect balance and control between these two required, and yet very different, disciplines.

If sales or marketing has too much control, the company will suffer. Without balance, neither discipline will reach their mutual goals and neither will the person who sits in the sales and marketing control chair. Without balanced sales and marketing efforts, the overall profit and growth margins of the company will not be reached.

At the point of the entrepreneurial start-up phase, everyone from the founder to the janitor is sales and marketing focussed. Ultimately, everyone knows that no one has a job until someone sells something to someone else! However, once the company is doing well, everyone is held accountable for reaching his or her projected growth numbers regardless of how difficult those numbers may be to achieve. The company will continue to replace whoever is in the VP of Sales and Marketing chair until the firm obtains the desired growth and profit objectives.

The very least this senior sales and marketing officer should consider is to hire a par level Director of Sales and a par level Director of Marketing reporting to the senior VP to create the needed balance. Ultimately, the senior VP's job longevity depends on his or her giving equal focus, effort, support, and resources to both of these uniquely different but critical disciplines.

If too much time, effort, and capital are invested on the marketing side of any firm, it becomes counterproductive. Sales managers and salespeople have a difficult time understanding and applying pure marketing logic. The sales force focus is placed on the corporate image and advertising and not on the delivery process, where it needs to be for sales to steadily increase.

Conversely, if too much emphasis is placed on the pure sales side of a company, the salespeople and sales managers start running the company. Administration, accounting, and delivery start being told what to do instead of being consulted.

Marketing people have an easier time blending with middle and upper management because their education and culturing is more compatible with corporate management. Marketing and administration are **intellectual** processes. Selling is an **emotional** process. Even though it is far easier for people educated in marketing to integrate and harmonize with home office management, an imbalance is still created. When marketing mindsets run companies, you hear HQ comments and phrases like, "This would be a perfect company to work for if it weren't for those salespeople!"

When the balance scale gets tipped too far on the sales side and people with pure sales backgrounds start running things you hear, "This would be a perfect company to work for if it weren't for the bean counters!"

Here is a Steven Lloyd-ism.

"The longer you remain in the field selling, the easier it appears to run companies. Conversely, the longer you remain out of the field, the easier it appears to sell what your company produces."

The best, most effective, and most profitable companies in the world have achieved a balance between sales and marketing management. Remember that Mr. Schwinn put bicycle pedals on opposing levels to create balance. It would not be long before you would wear yourself out trying to ride a bike with both pedals on the same side!

If you sell for a company that does not support you as a salesperson the way you believe you should be supported, you have three options. First, you can do nothing. This is not a great option. You will normally find yourself as chairperson of the "pity party." This is not much fun because you are normally the only one who comes to the party! It also creates a bigger division between sales and management. Even if your sales manager agrees that you are not being supported the way you should be, he or she will almost never side against upper management. They will not risk their job in an attempt to champion your cause. They're not against you, they are simply for themselves. There is a marked difference between the two.

Second, you can quit and go somewhere else. You might recognize the following phrase if you feel this way: "I was looking for a job when I found this one." If you really think that you'll find "Sales Heaven" somewhere else, you are kidding yourself. Whatever problems you have with this company you will simply take to or find at your next opportunity.

There is a great old story about a farmer working near a road that was being used by people migrating to his area. One crisp, fall morning he was working on his fence near the road when a wagon pulled up near him. The driver hailed the farmer and asked, "What kind of people live around here?" The farmer answered, "Well, what were the people like where you came from?" The traveler replied that they were a hard working and kind group of people. The farmer said, "Well, that is the kind of people you will most likely find here too." Several hours later a second wagon pulled up near where the farmer was working. The driver of this wagon asked the farmer the exact same question, "What kind of people live around here?" The farmer replied with the same question as he had to the earlier traveler, "Well, what were the people like where you came from?" The driver of the second wagon replied that they were a back-stabbing, negative group of people. The farmer responded, "Well, that is the kind of people you will most likely find here too."

So, if you quit and go somewhere else, you will probably find the same kinds of problems.

Third, you can create "Sales Heaven" right where you are! Regardless of who signs your paycheck, you are self-employed. Most World-Class salespeople have come to this same conclusion.

To enter "Sales Heaven," you must master both the marketing disciplines as well as the sales process. If you owned the company, you too would need to deliver your products and or services for the smallest possible cost without sacrificing quality, growth, or speed. As you start to think of yourself as self-employed, you will start to see yourself as working for yourself. You will also start to understand all of the elements that are required to succeed.

Thinking of yourself as self-employed will improve your life and career in more ways than you can currently imagine. You are now President and CEO of your own personal service sales and marketing company. The great news is that you do not have to develop the entire corporate infrastructure to deliver what you sell! You only have to build a sales and marketing "company." This is relatively simple compared to building the entire firm. Master the art and science of sales and marketing where you are now, and you will get to fill in the numbers on your own paycheck. The truth is, you have been filling the numbers in on your own paycheck all along.

BELIEVE it or not, everyone is on a commission. The fact is that every company must receive a three-for-one return for every dollar they pay out for income regardless of the form of payment. They must get back the dollar they paid out, a dollar for the taxes due on the revenue generated, and a dollar for profit. If a company does not get a minimum of three dollars back for every dollar they pay out in income, they will fire you. So, everyone is on a commission. A salary is not a base, it is a ceiling! With commission sales you earn exactly what you are worth. With a salary you can work just enough to not get fired or 80 hours a week, your income does not change.

Look at the salespeople who earn $100,000 or more per year. The majority have come to the conclusion that they are self-employed! The system is the same regardless of the company you sell for. So, let's take the first step towards getting you the results you want and need. It is called Bullseye Thinking!

CHAPTER TWO
Bullseye Thinking

CLEARLY DEFINING WHAT IT IS YOU REALLY WANT

Bullseye thinking is where it all begins. If you are not receiving the majority of what you want out of your life and career, this process will help you tremendously.

Most people have not clearly decided **exactly** what they want. How can your mind hit a target that you do not see? It clearly cannot, any more than you can shoot an arrow and hit a target that you cannot see! This chapter is critical if you want to arrive at the success level where you want and need to be. However, you must follow each step of this process. Even if you think you know the answers or have done other work similar to this, please do these exercises anyway. You may be surprised at what you learn. If you will do the exercises here, you will be amazed and delighted at how this chapter pulls your personal, professional, and economic pictures into a clearer success focus for you. With these exercises, and all of the exercises I offer you in this book, please stop reading when I ask you to and do each exercise. Remember that success is not an intellectual process. Success is an understanding that comes from doing. When you can do, you truly understand.

Exercise 1: Income

If this is your book then write in it. It's okay and necessary for you to make your notes here, in your book. If you borrowed this book, then get a notebook or journal to make your notes. You will need a new notebook or journal to do some of the upcoming work anyway so now would be a good time to pick one up if you do not already have one. Get a pen and let's get started!

In the past five years, what were your best three income years?

Best—year	(A)	$_____
Second-best-year	(B)	$_____
Third-best-year	(C)	$_____
Total	(D)	$_____
Divide three year total (D) by 3	(E)	$_____

Now that you have your highest three-year annual average income, multiply that number by 133% and enter that number on the line provided on line "F" below.

(F) $_____

This is now your **Bullseye Income Target** for the next 12 months! If this seems low, you can always adjust it higher *after* you hit your **Bullseye Income Target**. If it seems high, take a deep breath, let it out and relax. You will hit this **Bullseye Income Target** using what I am about to teach you!

Here is where you need to understand how the human mind works where income generation is concerned. I have been a sales manager for over a quarter of a century. I have hired, trained, and managed thousands of salespeople. I have conducted more goals-setting workshops than I can count. These experiences and observations have taught me that your brain will only accept a 33% increase in income over your highest three-year annual average, within the past five-year experience. The reason will become clear to you over the next few pages.

All human performance comes from your BELIEF system. Your BELIEFS are, in part, created by your experiences. Think about this question, "How far can you run without stopping?" Let's say that you know that you can run one mile. How do you know that you can run one mile?

You know that you can because you ran one mile recently. Now, what if I said, "I BELIEVE you can run five miles without stopping?" Regardless of how much enthusiasm I express about your ability to run five miles or how much pressure I put on you to agree with me, your brain would most likely say "No, I don't BELIEVE that I can run five miles." Why? Because you do not have a recent history of running more than one mile!

What if I said, "Well, you can run two miles can't you?" Your brain would probably say, "No, that's twice as far as I have ever run before, I don't BELIEVE I can run that far."

Even if I tried to persuade you to say the words, "Yes, I can run two miles," you still would not BELIEVE you could do it because you have no BELIEF that says you can do it based on a recent history of running anywhere even close to that far. You actually have a BELIEF that says, "I can't run two miles." You have this BELIEF because you have no recent history of running even close to that distance. If you could run two miles you would have done it, true? Even if I could get you to agree with me that you can run twice as far as you have in the past, you would probably leave my office feeling weak and defeated. After BELIEVING that I had "motivated" you to agree with me, I, as your sales manager, would probably be sitting in my office feeling very self-satisfied thinking I have accomplished a great deal with you because I got you to say the words, "I will run two miles!" Without a working knowledge of the human BELIEF system, I would not know that I had been ineffective because I would not understand that I had actually de-motivated you because I got you to say something that you do not BELIEVE. Contained within this example are both the problem and the solution.

Your running results, much like your unrealistic income goals, will remain about the same as they have been in your past experience. The only things that might change are the excuses you need to come up with to explain why you did not run the 100% farther distance that you promised.

Imagine if I coached and encouraged you with the following technique and strategy. What if I said to you, "I know, and you know, that you can run one mile, true? We know this because you've done it at least three times in the recent past. When you were done running one mile, did someone have to come and pick you up in the car or did you have a little more distance potential left in you?" You would most likely respond that you had a little more distance left in you. "One-third of a mile is only four additional average city blocks farther than you have a history of running. Do you think that you could run that same mile plus a little more, say four more blocks?" Most people would say, "Yes." We both know you can, the questions are, will your brain accept that you can and, will you at least try?

The word try, in this case, means complete and total willingness on your part. Willingness must come from you. Once you are completely and totally willing to do anything and everything that you need to do to succeed, the help you need always shows up. Running farther or selling more could require that you be more effective with the same effort. Being more effective at running might mean that you need new running shoes. You may need some coaching or breathing techniques to make you more effective. You can work hard—most of the people I speak to and talk with following my workshops all claim that they do work hard. There is however, a world of difference between effort and effectiveness.

The generation of your income works exactly the same way as far as your BELIEFS, discipline of your willpower, and your effectiveness are concerned.

Exercise 2: YOUR EFFECTIVENESS TO COMPENSATION RATIO

What percentage of your total effectiveness have you been investing towards your income? Here's where you must be totally honest with yourself. Circle the percentage next to the Bullseye Target graphic that most honestly describes your total effectiveness. Then, write that percentage number on the line provided. Remember that this is your book and no one else will ever see your answers so, please be totally honest with yourself. Also remember, I said effectiveness not effort. Admittedly, effectiveness is somewhat subjective. You have, however a fairly good idea what percentage your effectiveness is. If you don't know, ask your manager. They will be glad to tell you.

The Bullseye Effectiveness Formula

Bullseye	=	100%
2nd ring	=	90%
3rd ring	=	80%
4th ring	=	70%
5th ring	=	60%
Off Target	=	50%

_____ %

Answer

Now, multiply your three year income average from line [E] on page 32, by your Effectiveness Percentage and enter that number in the dollar sign line below.

$_____

Example: $100,000 (best three of five year income average) x 80% (or whatever your Effectiveness Percentage was) equals $80,000.

Do you see the relationship between effectiveness and earnings? How close did this formula come to your actual current income? It is rare for your income to significantly exceed your effectiveness. If it does, you need to go back and take a realistic look at your effectiveness.

Remember that if others in your organization are producing the numbers, you can too. If your numbers are less than theirs, look again at your effectiveness. If you are not being effective, this does not mean you are not trying. You may need help increasing your effectiveness. Please remember that you can run hard on a treadmill, but you are still just running in place. Here is another Steven Lloyd-ism.

"If you do not move from a stationary position, the scenery never changes!"

Do not confuse effort with effectiveness. Effectiveness is what moves you forward, improves your results, and allows you to make a difference, not just a living.

It is normal and typical for 100% effective salespeople to hit 100% of their Bullseye Income Targets. If you have been less than 70% effective and made more than 70% of your economic goal, you did not earn it! You will also not stay at that current income level very long.

You cannot change the base law of the universe, CAUSE and EFFECT. There is a fundamental problem with "coasting" or being "lucky" by being in the right place at the right time. The problem is that your forward progress slows down so gradually that you do not notice that you have lost momentum until it is too late. The best example of this that I know of is the sport of sculling. I am sure you have seen pictures of these athletes in those sleek one-person boats rowing along the mirror-smooth water of a bay. When the rower gets tired, he or she moves the oars into the boat to allow his or her arms to rest. The boat does not seem to slow down at all at first. The forward progress CAUSED by the rowing appears to remain the same as when the athlete was still rowing. The rower knows that this is not really true. They only rest long enough to gain enough strength to row again. As soon as they are rested, they take the oars in their hands again, time the stroke of the oars with the speed of the boat and start rowing again at their current speed. They know if they do not start rowing again that the boat will eventually slow down to the point that it will require more strength and effort to restart the boat than to maintain their current speed.

There is another universal law that governs all progress or motion. It says, *"An object in motion tends to stay in motion until acted on by an outside force."* However, that same law also says; *"An object at rest tends to stay at rest until acted on by an outside force."* Please allow the application of the **success systems** in this book to be your positive outside force! Please allow them to restart you or to keep you going and to increase your speed and success. Allow me to help you discover what you BELIEVE and to help you discover what is possible for you to achieve. I will coach you every step of the way, however you must do the work!

It does not matter if we are examining running or income generation, you must set a target that your brain BELIEVES it can hit if you want to succeed. If you do not BELIEVE that the income target is attainable it is like starting a race that you BELIEVE you cannot win. If you feel defeated or dejected before you start, you will not put your whole Heart into any effort or endeavor and you will never really start. You can do a little more. You can run a little farther. You can make a few more sales calls, which will result in more presentations, which will CAUSE more sales. You really can! However, doubling your income in one year is not realistic and your brain knows it!

Ask yourself this question: If your highest three-year annual average income over the past five years was $100,000 per year, would you expect another company to offer you $200,000 a year for the same effectiveness? You know you would not expect a 100% increase. It would be nice, but not realistic. You can hope they offer you 50% more, but we both know if it was your company and your money, you would not offer that much unless you were seeking a rare and difficult to find person to fill a critical position. These offers are rare.

On the other hand ask yourself this question: If you were satisfied with both the company you work for and the compensation you are currently receiving, would you consider leaving your current company for $100,000 if you were presently making $100,000? Of course not! How would you feel if I offered you $120,000? Notice how I am starting to get both your attention and your interest. How does $133,000 sound to you? Notice how you BELIEVE that this amount of increase is possible for you to receive.

I have personally worked this 33% increase formula with hundreds of salespeople for many years, very successfully. It is possible for you too, and the great news is that you do not have to go anywhere else to get it! You can increase your income by one-third right here where you are, starting now! You also can increase it by 33% year after year. Your increase in income will be effective as soon as you are! In addition to effectiveness you must also be consistent. You have to keep "pumping" all day, everyday!

When I was a kid on the farm, we had an old hand water pump. To get water for the cattle we had to "prime the pump" with the very thing we wanted from the well, and that was water! When the leathers that were attached to the rod inside the pump shaft were "primed" by the water poured down the top of the pump, they swelled. The expansion caused a vacuum in the pipe. This vacuum CAUSED the positive pressure needed so we could draw water up from the well, into the pipe, out the spout, and into the watering tank for the cattle.

I remember to this day how much hard work it was to get the water all the way up the pipe. Once the water started flowing, all that was required was steady and consistent pumping to keep the water flowing. Compared to the effort to get the water up the pipe and flowing, the pumping effort was easy! As soon as I stopped pumping, the most amazing thing happened, the water did not stop flowing right away! The water flow decreased slowly at first and then eventually stopped. I could actually hear the water going back down the pipe as the vacuum CAUSED by the pumping was lost. The longer I waited to start the pumping process again, the farther the water went down the pipe and the harder I had to work to get the water flowing again.

This metaphor is also true about your life and your sales career. The dollars cannot keep flowing if the sales stop. The sales will not happen if the presentations are not made. The presentations will not happen if the appointments are not set. The appointments will not get set if you or someone else does not make the appointment-setting calls. You cannot make the calls if you do not have leads. You cannot have leads if you do not have prospects. You cannot have prospects if you do not have suspects. You cannot have suspects if you do not know where to look. So, let's move on to the next step of World-Class sales performance-**Prospecting!**

CHAPTER THREE
PROSPECTING

ACRES OF DIAMONDS

A suspect is someone who has the possibility of buying what you sell. Notice I said possibility. Suspecting is doing the research to find your prospects. A prospect is someone who has the likelihood of buying what you sell. Neither suspects nor prospects are leads.

A lead is defined, at least in this work, as a prospect for whom you have all of the critical information needed, including a reason to contact him or her. As far as I know, this is the purest definition of a lead. Depending on your budget and time, the degree by which you qualify each lead is up to you. Remember that if your company had thousands of people "waiting in line" to buy what you sell, they would not need salespeople!

Where do you find prospects? There are two major sources. First, look within the list of satisfied clients (customers and clients are synonymous in this book) of your firm, as referrals. Second are people or companies that have a similar profile to the existing clients of your firm. Those clients fall into one of two categories. These categories are business-to-business or business-to-consumer. Either way, remember this Steven Lloyd-ism.

"Birds of a feather buy products and or services together."

Write that phrase down on a 3x5 card. Insert the word or words of the products and or service you sell where I use the words "products and or services," and carry this card with you to remind you of the "Acres Of Diamonds" that are all around you.

Russell Conwell became world famous for telling the story of Acres of Diamonds. You may recall the story of an African farmer who became mesmerized by the shiny gemstones called diamonds. He was so infatuated with these stones that were bringing such high prices on the world markets that he sold his farm to search for diamonds. After years of looking and looking, in a fit of depression he committed suicide.

One day, the man who bought his farm was walking across one of his fields and stumbled over a rock. He turned the rock over and was fascinated by the crystal-like formation of the stone. He brought the rock back to his house, cleaned it up, and placed it on his fireplace mantel as a conversation piece. One night, the new owner of the farm and his wife invited some people over for dinner. After dinner the men went into the living room, as was the custom of the day, to discuss whatever men talked about in those days. One of the guests looked at the stone on the fireplace mantel and said, "Where did you find a diamond of this size?" The farmer remarked, "This is not a diamond, a diamond is a beautiful gem, this is just a shiny rock, my farm is covered with them." His guest said, "Sir, I have studied diamonds for many years and this is what a diamond in its rough state looks like."

The new owner of this farm became one of the wealthiest men in the world because his farm turned out to be one of the largest and richest diamond mines to ever be discovered, anywhere in the world.

One man sold a diamond mine to go looking for diamonds and died in despair. Another man met someone who showed him what diamonds in the rough state look like and became fabulously wealthy. I suggest that you too are sitting on "Acres Of Diamonds" just waiting for you to mine them.

If you are in direct sales to a personal or residential market, find out what neighborhoods or general locations have already bought from your company. Make a list of those satisfied buyers. Do not call them, *go to see them!* You sell for a firm that falls into one of two categories: single product or service or multiple products or services. If you have more than one "thing" for sale, start your interview with one of your firm's satisfied customers with what they like about what they already own that they bought from your company. Then, with your other products or services in mind that you know might satisfy them, start asking questions that relate to their other needs.

Keep them on what I call the *10/30-Power Formula* for success. Every ten days mail them a handwritten note using the Image Transfer System, which I will explain later, and every 30 days call them on the telephone or visit them in person. Remember that everyone prefers to keep buying from people they know and like rather than buying from strangers.

An example from my own selling history may help you see what is possible for you and your career. As I give you my history and explain the systems I have developed, see yourself and what you sell in the scenarios. The product or service is not what is important here. The system and the results are what counts!

When I started as a salesperson for a large insurance company, I was given a territory. I reviewed the files of all of the existing clients in my territory. I copied down 25 names, addresses, and telephone numbers to contact in my first week.

I called the 25 existing clients to introduce myself as their new agent and attempted to set an appointment to review their existing coverage. I received nine appointments for the 25 contacts that I made. Even though these people were existing clients of my company, they had not seen an agent for a long time and they seemed a little uncomfortable setting an appointment with someone they did not know. My "cold" call also seemed to catch them a little off guard.

The next week I sent a handwritten note to another 25 of the existing clients in the same territory, introducing myself as their new agent and letting them know I would be calling them. Then I called them to attempt to set appointments. Sending the "warm up" note made a big difference in the reception I received on the telephone because it gave me a reason to call. Many of the prospects said, "We were waiting for your call!" I increased my appointment setting ratio to 19 out of 25. Big increase, wouldn't you agree? This was the beginning of the **success system** you will learn about later.

Once I had the appointment, my initial strategy was to do a basic review of their existing coverage with our firm. Much like existing customers of most companies, they had not seen anyone from our firm in a long time. Many had never seen anyone after their original purchase. I upgraded over half of everyone of all I saw to a better policy. They were delighted to see me!

In the first 30 days of following just this one system, it put me in the top 10% of sales producers of a very large local agency.

Then an idea occurred to me. What if I was to perform the same service for all of the other insurance agents, for all of the other companies who did not call back to service their clients? After all, most salespeople, even today, are more focused on making new sales to new people than servicing their existing accounts. It worked like magic!

The challenge I had is much like the prospecting problems today. I will bet that when you even mention the fact that you sell something, like insurance, you see or feel a "wall" go up, true? What I discovered was that when I asked them, "who handles your insurance," they always had an answer. One day I asked, "Who is your Estate Financial Adviser?" It worked great! They had no idea what an Estate Financial Adviser was or did. This gave me the opportunity to explain my services while their mind was still open.

Each time I met someone new, regardless of where we met, I always asked him or her the same question, "Who is your Estate Financial Adviser?" They almost never had an answer. Then, I explained the organizational services I preformed for my existing clients and offered to do the same for them, free of charge.

I created a simple inventory form listing every policy they owned, so that they would have a record of it. I asked for and received every policy they owned. After listing each policy, name of company, agent's name and the contact information, I asked for my prospective client's permission to give them a receipt for their policies so I could review them. I promised to report back in a few days with a complete review, including a complete cost-versus-benefits analysis. With very few exceptions, each prospective client was delighted for me to do exactly that!

With a detailed review of each of their policies and a comparison of what I offered as coverage, I was able to replace a large percentage of their old policies. I increased their coverage and my sales dramatically. I was also a very active student of the life and health insurance business. In one of my "advanced field underwriting classes," (a fancy term for sales training), I learned a startling statistic that was at least valid then. Over 20% of all life insurance policies issued are never collected on at the insured's death. Guess why? No one ever knew they owned the policy and that the insured person had died! Thousands of policies have cash value to carry the premium for years! After the policy runs out of cash, the person no longer lives at their old address and the premium notice is sent back to the insurance company and finally lapses for nonpayment of premiums. In those days it was also common for policies to be kept in a lock box at a bank that no one knew about except the person who died. Not a great plan!

I also noticed that every time I would stop by just to help my health insurance clients handle a claim, they really appreciated my service. I started to feel like family. I almost always received referrals from them. I designed a referral generating **success system** that can be applied to whatever you sell. Wait until you see how simple yet powerful it is!

One day, in a creative moment, I asked one of my married couple clients what they would do if something happened to both of them at the same time, like, a car crash? I asked who they would want to have informed about their business affairs, insurance, wills, trusts, etc? The most amazing thing happened. **Nothing!** They did not have a clue. They sat there and looked at me like a "tree full of owls." They had never even thought about it!

I continued to ask client after client the same question. I got almost the same response from each one. Then, about a week after I started this research project I got another clue from one of my clients when I asked a similar question. She said, "Would you be willing to do that for us? After all, you have all of our health and life insurance records now!"

I said, "Yes, however I would need a list of all of your assets including all of your insurance and financial documents." Then the husband spoke up and gave me another major piece to the new prospecting puzzle.

He said, "Maybe we should make a list of everything and give it to our lawyer and CPA now, before something happens to one or both of us." I thought, "What a brilliant idea! In fact, I can do this as an additional service for all of my clients. Then, when something does happen, there is no added burden on family members because of wondering what to do next." **It worked great!**

This is how my **success system** works. Remember to look at this system and see what you might do to apply the ideas to whatever you sell. I know you will see a similar avenue of possibility for yourself if you use your creative imagination. Several of my students are already using modifications of this **success system** and have increased their sales dramatically!

I explained to each prospective client the benefit of having loved ones and other advisers informed of their wishes prior to death or when needed. It was simple and easy for them to see the value of having one person acting as the "Trustee," holding the files along with their insurance papers, financial records, and final requests.

We agreed that I would keep a copy of all financial documents in their file at my office. I made a backup copy for each client to have in case something happened to me. Also, I agreed to contact both their attorney and CPA, if they had one, to explain the arrangement and request that I be notified by them when anything happened to my clients in case the accountant or lawyer happened to be contacted first.

Now the family, their executor, or attorney would only have to make one call to have access to the insurance records, client files, financial records, and the client's final requests. Legal permission was given in their Will with a Client Instructions and Permission form, which I kept a copy of in my file.

I prepared a simple but professional 8½ x 11 Insurance, Asset and Financial Records form. With each prospective client I asked the same "What if" questions and received almost the same looks and answers from each. I explained what other clients had asked me to do for them. I offered to do the same for my new clients after I had reviewed, replaced, updated, and organized their insurance files.

The golden key to remember here is that I was already liked, BELIEVED, and trusted because I had already performed a valuable service for him, her, or them: reviewing, advising, organizing, and replacing their insurance files and policies.

Almost without exception, each client wanted me to perform the same service. Many offered to pay me for it. I explained that it would be my pleasure to help them and that they could reward me by telling their friends and relatives about the services I had performed for them.

Remember that the records shared with their other advisers, relatives, and friends did not disclose any of the facts of my client's assets or financial matters, just the fact that I was the person to call when something happened to my client. Informing their relatives and other advisers of this planning is an important part of this prospecting **success system**.

Part of the process of creating the file was the need for the names, addresses, and telephone numbers of their relatives, trusted friends, legal and accounting advisers. They willingly gave me this information. I then put my name in the client's Rolodex and telephone books under insurance, financial, and under my name. I was the first person I know of to convert my business card to magnetic material and put it on their refrigerator. Now there is a peel-off magnetic material available so you can convert your card into one, too.

As I stated earlier, in the very first week as a new agent, I moved into the top 10% of sales producers in a very large local agency by just calling on former clients and updating their existing policies. Within 90 days of using the **success system** I am teaching you now, I moved into the top 1% of national sales producers for the entire company, which automatically put me into the top 10% of my industry! Again, this information is not to impress you but to impress upon you that it is the **success system** that made it happen!

My next step in the development of this **success system** was to call and set a meeting with the family members, close friends, legal and accounting advisers of my clients. This meeting was set as having only one purpose and that was to advise them what to do when something happened to my client. No one refused me because even though I made the call, my client requested the meeting!

I had a simple but well-organized file folder professionally printed and always brought one with me to show each prospective client a sample of the kind of file I was keeping for their friend, relative, or client.

The file has a section for listing all of the insurance policies of each client as well as all of the other types of assets listed by section. Each section provides space to list all of the companies and all of the agents with their names and phone numbers.

As I reviewed the generic form with my client's friend, relative, or other adviser, it was a simple matter to demonstrate the value of this type of planning. My client's actual file, which was never disclosed to anyone, now had an updated and current list of assets and contact information. My name, address, and phone number was at the top of the list in bold print on both the sample as well as the actual file.

I reviewed all of the "what if" scenarios and explained that all of the details and wishes had been worked out with my client. I showed them a sealed file that contained a copy of their Will and all of their financial documents. Everything was ready for the day when they would be needed.

Most of my clients wanted their accountant and attorney to have copies of their insurance information. The CPA got a copy of the insurance information and some minor references on the legal matters that each client had approved. The CPA already had all of the accounting files. The accountants were as eager as the attorneys to get a copy of the insurance information. The lawyers almost always wanted a copy of everything! They were only given the same information the CPA received unless my client advised me to give them what they requested.

One of my students took this **success system** to a new level of service. As this process developed and progressed for him, he helped his clients work out the details of their final wishes, funeral services, and expenses. After several months of working with my **success system**, he called on all of the funeral directors in his entire marketplace. He explained my system. The funeral directors were all very impressed. He learned that almost all funeral directors have prearranged, prepaid final expense plans that take care of every detail of the funeral expenses and services.

Even though their fees did not change, he received a handsome commission for setting up everything in advance with his clients. This worked out well for the funeral directors, too, because most people do not think about these issues until they are very old or there is a death in the family. My **success system** brought new revenue into their funeral home businesses years before they expected it. They were happy and even desirous of paying my student a fair commission. It helped the funeral director's business and it benefited my student's clients, in many ways.

Because he had all of the funeral homes under contract, his clients got to pick which service and facility they wanted to use. Their decisions were normally based on personal experience with the funeral home or religious motivations. Only if they had no preference would my friend make recommendations based on location to family members, size of the facility, etc. He made sure his personal compensation was always the same with each facility so that money was never a motivation behind his input.

Here is a Steven Lloyd-ism.

> **"***If* you *always* focus on what serves the client, your needs will *always* be met!"**

One of the secrets of my **success system** was that only the details that each client wanted shared with other people was ever disclosed. What I could share and could not share with others was always clearly written out and signed by both my clients and myself. If the family member, friend, or adviser asked a question that my client did not want disclosed, I would simply say, "I'm sorry, that information is sealed!" Many would ask, but that statement always stopped their inquiries.

After my review of the information that my client wanted shared with each of the people important to my client, which normally took about 45 minutes, I asked each of the relatives, friends, or advisers, "Do you have your insurance and financial affairs organized this well?" Almost without exception each one said, "No." All I had to do at that point was say, "As long as I'm here, please go get your insurance policies and let's start this same process for you now! There is no charge for the service. All my fees are paid by the insurance and financial companies you select."

It is important for you to understand that because I had invested the time to help a person that they really cared about, I now had rapport and trust built with them. Helping them prepare for a sad and emotional time in the future was very much appreciated. Almost 70% of them let me perform the same service for them.

Remember also, most people, even today, do not have their financial affairs in order. Even with financial planners, attorneys, and accountants on almost every corner and all of them offering to help, a huge need remains unfulfilled. Even with the software stores and the Internet bursting with estate planning software, the vast majority of people still do not have their financial affairs well planned. Why is this? The answer is so simple it will amaze you. They really do not think they are going to die or they BELIEVE that they will die but not until they are very old. The vast majority of families have not taken care of their planning needs. There is a fortune to be made for those planning professionals who will make easy, simple, and respectful what is difficult, complex, and painful for people to deal with or face.

For those who embraced my help I proceeded to get their financial affairs in order. After I had all of their insurance policies organized, I did something they did not expect. I did not try to sell them anything! The majority would ask me what I thought about their insurance. I would always say, "I don't know. I need to review each policy to see if you're getting the best possible value. As long as we have all of your policies out, let me give you a receipt for them, take them back to my office and study them for you. What day next week is best in your schedule for us to get together and review what I have discovered?" At that point, almost all of them set an appointment and the majority bought policies from me.

This is when I started to develop the "**Getting Hired vs Closing The Sale**" sales technique. Somewhere in this process, I discovered a powerful phrase. Adjusted for what you do, this phrase will work for you too. Mine was, "I am applying for the job as your Estate Financial Adviser." It worked so well because none of them had an Estate Financial Adviser. They did not know what an Estate Financial Adviser was. This worked well because they had no preconceived "picture" in their minds and thus, no BELIEFS about it. Because they had no "picture" in their minds, they had no "box" in which to place me. I was not competing with someone they BELIEVED was performing the same or similar service. All you need to do is redefine what your title is to what you really want to accomplish for the client, then use that as your title.

By the next week I had studied all of their insurance policies and prepared a cost/value proposal on each policy. The majority of these second-generation prospects became clients for the same reasons their friends, relatives, or advisers did. The same referral system was employed with them that introduced me to them in the first place and my **success system** continued to create more generations of clients and referrals.

As time went by, I developed a relationship with a good casualty insurance agent to analyze the homeowners and automobile policies that I did not sell. By working with me and analyzing the casualty insurance policies that I did not offer, this agent friend of mine wrote many of my clients new homeowners and auto insurance policies. Because this **success system** worked so well, he opened his files to me and asked me to perform the same services for his clients.

We had a written agreement that I was the Adviser of record for all of my clients and he was the Adviser of record for all of his clients. The agreement clearly spelled out that I controlled all of the flow of all of the contacts to my clients and he controlled all of the flow of all of the contracts to his clients.

When you develop a relationship with another vendor that does what you do not, remember to have a written agreement with them. It is critical, however, that you maintain complete control of the relationship with your clients. This same concept and **success system** will work for whatever you sell. Most likely you do not sell everything your client needs. Even in your general area of expertise there are most likely several products and or services that your clients need that they cannot get from you. However, in the general areas of what you do sell, you can and must become your client's adviser! In the areas of what you do not sell, you can be the contact for them to get what they need, through you.

Find another salesperson to do what you do not do and you will become the resource each customer needs to solve his or her larger needs. Look at your general area of products or services and ask yourself, "Who else can I use as a 'consultant' to expand my value to each of my clients?" Expand your ability to serve and you expand your value. Expand your value and you will dramatically increase your sales! Build relationships and the sales will be a natural effect! If you continue to look for more ways to just "dump" more "stuff" to make more commissions, you will continue to struggle forever!

I promised you that I would show you both the "business-to-business" and "business-to-consumer" approach. Remember your Steven Lloyd-ism,

"*Birds of a feather buy products and or services together!*"

Let's start with the assumption that you have at least one business client. Call your local library and ask if they have a CD-ROM system called American Business Disk by InfoUSA. If not, call several libraries and see if you can find it.

If you cannot find it in your area, ask if they have the Dunn & Bradstreet Business Directory, or Microcosm. Microcosm is an older system that uses microfiche viewing files. Some of the smaller libraries still have this system. All of these systems are great because they list all of the businesses by Standard Industry Code (SIC). This is great because all of the files are organized by industry, company, and ZIP code.

Let's say you sell "widgets" to commercial businesses. Look up your current customer(s) in the SIC directory to determine in which general category your customer falls. Next, look at a ZIP code map, which is also available at your local library. Find your ZIP code. Work a ring of ZIP codes around where you live or work. Write down all of the ZIP codes closest to you. Working close to your home or office saves time and money!

Next, go to the ZIP code file for all of the SIC business codes with the same SIC as your customer. Remember each listing shows the name of the company, the address, the telephone numbers, the name of the owner or manager, the number of employees, and what they do or sell. This **success system** will supply you with all of the information you need to convert these suspects into prospects. Treat each one with the respect they deserve because these prospects become leads. I will show you how to convert these leads into appointments and how to convert those appointments into new customers!

Regardless of the format that you use to gather your names, be sure you have at least 250 prospect records from which to start. The American Business Disk system is an easier and less expensive system to use. Most libraries will let you bring your own disk and copy files for free!

There is only one major drawback. The information in these files changes frequently. This service is provided to your library for a very low cost. It is not possible to keep these files as up-to-date or to provide as high a quality of leads. In just six months, almost 25% of the names and contact information will have changed. That number doubles to almost 50% in just one year.

I have had so many requests for us to design and manage this for our sales, marketing, and management training and education clients that we now offer current, up-to-date, and verified leads for almost every industry or company in the USA. All of our leads are contacted on an ongoing basis to make sure the information is fresh and up-to-date. We do a huge volume so we can provide the leads for less cost than you could get on your own. Our leads also provide you with a lot more information than the library offers and all of the information is current and correct!

We are not in the leads or data sales business. We are in the Human Engineering and sales development business. Like other products and services we provide our clients, we make it simple and easy for you to call one source and get most of your sales results needs satisfied. When you and your business are at the "We have some extra money to invest in leads" stage, you will be amazed what can be done for $1,000! Do not concern yourself with this now. When the value of your time exceeds the value of the cost of having your leads generated for you, just call us. You will know when you are ready for our help in this area.

I suggest that you test the system through the library and then, after you are convinced of the value and have the capital, call us and order our **success system** to be used on a larger and more sophisticated scale. You will find as your business grows that the investment of some capital for more detailed and up-to-date leads is well worth the investment. We provide sales contact leads for just about any kind of industry or company you can imagine. We can also show you how to use the information in the latest contact software programs. Here again, this is for future reference. My objective here is to show you how to use little or no money and convert research and a little effort into high quality leads.

This will be the first and last time I will ask you to call us or visit our web site to investigate the products or services we have developed and offer. I do not want it to appear that I am weaving several commercial messages throughout this book regardless of how much I know they will benefit you. Each time, from now on, I will mention only the product or service as it relates to what I am teaching you. The only reminder I will print is, (If you want to learn more, see the Resources Section in the back of this book). It will be up to you to follow up with my office if you want to learn more.

My **success system** is based on you having more leads than you can possibly work! When you have more leads than you can possibly work, you will have a whole different attitude about approaching too many leads. When you have only a few leads, you tend to hoard those precious few leads. Imagine 250 people standing in line waiting to see you! Good feeling isn't it?

Once you have your 250+ records, it is time to go back to your office. Next, convert all of the individual listings on the pages to separate 5x7 index cards. Each step of this **success system** is important. Make sure you use 5x7 index cards. It is important that you write the information on the 5x7 card in pencil because you will need to erase some of the managers' names and some of the other information that has changed. As you call to verify the information, put a checkmark by the information that is correct and erase and replace the information that is not. The check mark will remind you later that you did, indeed, verify the information. Also, put a date in the upper left-hand corner so you will know when the date you verified this information. Even if you use a computer contact system to track your leads, please follow these instructions.

Now you are ready to call all of the prospect cards, and here is what you say to the person who answers the telephone. "Hi, this is (your name), what is your name? Hi (their name). I am updating my business files and I need to verify some information. Are you still located at (address printed on your card)? Good, is (name of owner/manager) still there?" You will notice that the managers and owners will change but companies and their important contact information stay fairly consistent. As you verify or obtain the new manager's name, use a green highlighter to highlight the current manager or owner's name.

Next say, "Is he or she still the person responsible for buying (your products or services)?" About 50% of the time they will tell you who is responsible or refer you to someone who can tell you. Close your conversation with this: "(Their name), this is (your name), thank you for helping me! I am just curious, what's your favorite color?" When they tell you what their favorite color is, say, "Oh, I like that color too! Thanks again for helping me. Have a great day! Goodbye."

By repeating their name and your name at least twice in your brief conversation and noting their favorite color, you can call them by name and remind them of their favorite color when you call back to set your appointment. If you took the time to build the proper rapport, they will remember you! We all like to help people that we like. Always remember the importance of the "care and feeding" of the gatekeepers! They control whether you move on to the decision-maker or not.

It is very important that you make all of the calls and update all of your prospect cards before you go on to the next step. You will also notice that you will overcome most if not all of your fear of the telephone by using this very low rejection **success system**.

The next step is to call your client and invite him or her to lunch. Try saying something like this; "I want to buy you lunch and get to know you better. Which day this week looks most open in your calendar for us to enjoy 60 minutes, breaking bread together?" Suggest that you go early, around 11:00 a.m. or late, around 1:00 p.m. so you can have a little quiet time to talk and avoid the noon rush. When you set your lunch appointment, be sure to ask, "Do you have at least an hour so we can visit as well as eat?" If they say "No" ask, "What day this week do you have an hour for me?" You need at least an hour!

I like 11:00 a.m. for business lunches, because restaurants are past their breakfast crowd rush and by the time the lunch crowd comes in you are finished with your lunch. You also get the best service with the fewest interruptions.

Bring all of your new prospect cards with you but do not take them out during the first 15 minutes of your lunch. To build rapport quickly, ask open-ended questions to get your client talking. Those open-ended questions start with who, what, where, when, why, and how?

Everyone feels better and likes you more when they get to talk about their favorite subject: themselves! Keep the conversation light. Never crack jokes or use slang or profane language, even if they do. You never know if you are being tested. Even if you feel very close to this person, always keep your language professional! No one will ever buy from you because you told an off-color joke or story or used bad language. However, many will not buy from you because you did! If your client likes to tell jokes and they ask, "Have you heard this one" say, "I'm not sure, tell it anyway!" Then act as if you have not heard it and laugh at the punch line! One of the fastest ways to build rapport is to be a good audience.

Here are some good, time-tested, rapport building questions to start the client talking. Even though you like to talk, remember the name of the game is to get and keep the client talking! Also, don't forget to keep in mind to start your personal questions slow and easy and build up to the more flattering and informational questions.

Try starting with:

- So (client's first name), how long have you owned or been associated with (name of their company)? What did you do before that?
- How did you get into (whatever their company does)?
- Where do you see your firm going in the next three years?
- What do you see yourself doing within those changes, personally?

Now it is time to start learning about them personally. The last question leads you into this process naturally because you used the word, "personally." The next question will test how open they will be with you.

If they do not open up to you about their personal life, do not push it! They may choose to keep their personal life just that, personal.

- You seem to be a really dedicated person. How does your diligence affect your personal life?

This is the point that you are looking for them to drop the name of a spouse, significant other, or the names of their children.

As they talk, mentally review, spell, and picture other people in your mind with the same names as those they referenced in their conversation. Later, you will record those relationships and names on their 5x7 client card. As they are talking, keep a picture in your mind of someone else you know who has the name of their spouse, significant other, or children's names so you can "burn" their name into your memory. You will find that this technique makes it easy for you to recall the names of those people closest to your client whenever you need to. Never write the names down in front of your client. If they open up to you about their family, use the open-ended question technique to gain more information.

- So, how long have you and (spouse or significant other's name) been together?
- How old is (child's name)?

One of the most memorable things you will ever do for anyone is remember their birthday and the birthdays of the people they care about. The following technique will help you determine what their birthday is without running the risk of asking how old they are.

- I'm just curious, what is your birth sign?

Only a small fraction of people have strong BELIEFS about astrology. Most everyone will tell you what his or her birth sign is. If you find that your friend is negative, you can lead into the birth sign technique like this: "I do not put much stock in astrology, do you?" Intelligent business people will normally say, "No." Then say, " They say I'm an Aries (or whatever your birth sign is). To me, most of the horoscopes look the same. I'm just curious, what sign are you?" They will normally tell you. Then go on to the next question.

- Interesting, what month and day were you born?

Remember, never ask the year! Normally, they will tell you. Make a mental note of it by picturing the month in your mind. Spell the month and recall anything else that happens in that same month. Then count to yourself one through the number of the day that they were born. Later you can record this information on your 5x7 client card.

Be one of the important friends who sends them a birthday card. Everyone likes to be remembered!

It is likely that your client also has good communication skills. Be prepared for them to ask you questions. Answer the question and come back with another question that is related to their question. You will most likely notice that their question will be related to the questions that you have asked them. If they continue to ask you questions, regain control by answering their question and asking another question that is not related to the series of questions that you are asking each other. You might ask, "Do you follow any of the local sports teams?" or, "So how is business?"

Be aware of your time. After approximately 30 minutes, it is time to position yourself for them to help you. The three best ways I have discovered to enlist someone in helping you are to ask a favor, tell a secret or ask their opinion. The best way is to do all three at the same time.

Try this **success system**, the results will amaze and delight you! Say, "(Client's first name), let me tell you a secret." Lean forward, lower your voice and say, "I have decided to become the number one salesperson in my division. I want it kept a secret because the other sales people are very competitive. If they learn that I am taking a run at the number one spot, it will trigger their competitive nature and make it harder for me to win. So, I need to keep a low profile and prepare my sales and marketing strategy, and I need your help. I need your opinion on who the best prospects are in your industry. Will you help me?" In most cases, your client will express willingness to help you. Many will appear eager to help!

Next, you need to give them a reason for your need for help. Try this, "I have been reading Steven Lloyd's book, *Selling From The Heart*, and he says that there are 'Acres of Diamonds' right in my back yard. He said I should go to the library and pull all of the names of companies that do what your company does. Then he said that I should call on friends that I already have as customers to see if they know any of these other leaders."

Pull out your prospect cards, hand them to your new friend and say, "Do you know any of these other managers from these other companies?"

Be quiet and let him or her sort through the cards. When they come to a person they do know, set that card aside into a separate pile. Even if they want to tell you about them, it is important for him or her to go through the entire stack first. If your total stack of cards looks enormous, you may want to give him or her only half of the stack at first so that they will not be overwhelmed with the size of the pile.

You will notice that your new business friend will focus on the manager's name that is highlighted in green. You will now see the importance of highlighting the manager or owner's name with the green highlighter pen. I told you that this was a complete **success system**!

Please know and trust that this is a tested **success system** that will produce the desired results. However, you must follow each step exactly as I describe it. Every step is important, including the green color of the highlighter pen is important. If you have not recognized it already, very soon you will see that every step of this **success system** is important. Green represents *go*, red means *stop*, and yellow means *caution*. Our subconscious minds are receiving messages all of the time. What message do you want to send? The little things all add up to the big difference! Most of this **success system** operates at the subconscious level. We have already gotten closer to the customer's Heart, but we first have to complete the process of demonstrating value to his or her mind.

The next step is to go back through the stack of cards where your new business friend recognized the owner or manager's name.

Take the stack of cards back from your friend and repeat the name of the person they recognized and say, "What can you tell me about (name of the owner or manager)?" Turn the card over and write what they tell you. You will soon see why you need to use the 5x7 cards. You will need more writing room to write than 3x5 cards provide.

Here are some other important questions to ask. Notice I am now moving to asking closed-ended questions. Closed-ended questions can be answered with a simple, "yes" or "no."

- "Does (name of the owner or manager) know who you are?"
- "Do you belong to any professional, civic, or athletic groups together?"
- "Is this the person I should be calling on?"

- "Do you or they belong to any trade associations?"
- "Do you know if they are married or have kids?"

Here is where you want fast "yes" or "no" answers. This allows you to find the important information quickly with the least amount of dialogue. Remember that the clock is ticking! You may or may not want to ask some of these questions depending on how well they know this person. If they really do know them well, you will know it because he or she will say something like, "Yes, I know this person really well!" Create the following code for each of your prospect cards:

A = They know them well
B = They know them
C = They have heard of them
D = They don't know them at all

Next, ask, "Would it be okay with you for me to tell this person that we are friends and do business together?" Take out a blank card and ask, "Do you know anyone else from any other business or industry that I should be calling on?" Don't be surprised if they don't know or can't think of anyone else or they refer you back to your own list. This is a valuable question because they might know someone else and because their brain has been focused on the people that they know, you might get a great lead!

After you have gone through all of the cards and gathered your research, take out the cards where your client recognized people from his or her same industry and ask, "If you were me, who would you call first?" Based on their response, put a 1, 2, 3, or 4 on the card, following your A, B, C, D code.

You are now ready to move your personal and professional importance to the next level with your new business friend. Ask, "(Client's first name), what do you need to see, hear, or experience from me, for you to award me 100% of your business?" Allow him or her to think, respond, or do whatever he or she needs to do or say. It does not really matter because, the question is designed so that he or she understands that you are willing to do whatever it takes to earn 100% of his or her business.

This is an extremely powerful and effective technique. It works like magic! You may be in an industry where your new business friend is required to get bids and place the business with the lowest bidder.

You may already know if your client's company has a preferred vendor's list. If not, even with a very small company, ask, "Do you have a preferred vendor's list?" If they say, "Yes," ask, "What are the requirements to get on that list?" If they say, "No," ask, "Would you like for me to help you design a preferred vendor's list system, based on the same criteria used by the most successful companies in the world?" If they say, "Yes," say, "It will be my pleasure to do that for you. I will get it to you next week!"

All you need to do is call any public company and ask them for a copy of their preferred vendor's list requirements. You may have to call more than one company to get what you need but remember that public companies are required to disclose this information. Put together a sample of these requirements and send it to your client.

Always send everything of importance by an overnight shipping service. It makes your friend feel important. That feeling of importance is associated with and transferred to you. Find an overnight shipping service that looks good from the way that they dress to the vehicles that they drive. I prefer to use FedEx Express Saver service. Depending on where the delivery is, FedEx often gets the package there the next day for the price of their third business day express saver service. It is relatively inexpensive and it always puts me in the category of World-Class!

All of the overnight shipping service companies now have regional pricing. This means that your local or nearby deliveries now cost you less money! FedEx Express Saver service will get your important "image" packages delivered within three business days at the longest, and normally the next business day, locally. Remember you are building a long-term relationship. Never, and I mean never, appear cheap! I have used every overnight shipping service available and FedEx is the best by far. They treat you as if you are one of the most important customers, even if you ship only a few packages a year. Their couriers dress and present themselves professionally and therefore represent you in the best possible light.

The other reason we use FedEx exclusively is because of their World-Class service. One year at Christmas, I sent a case of specially designed coffee mugs filled with foil-covered chocolates to my managing associate in southern California for her to distribute to my associates as holiday gifts. My assistant shipped the case by FedEx as normal. The next day I asked if the box had arrived yet. I was told that it would not be there until day after tomorrow. I asked, "Why three days?" My assistant said, "I always ship supplies by third business day express saver!" I said, "Do you have any idea what the temperature is in a warehouse in southern California and what happens to chocolate over 80 degrees?" I received one of those "Oh my word" looks. I asked for the shipping bill and called 800-GO-FedEx. I spoke to a delightful lady named Jill and explained my situation. As soon as I gave her the tracking number I could hear her keying in the information. As soon as I finished what I was saying she politely said, "Good news Mr. Lloyd, your package is still on the truck. I have diverted it to its destination. It will be delivered within the hour, NO EXTRA CHARGE, Merry Christmas!"

This is only one of several wonderful experiences I have had with FedEx so I know the CAUSE must be their training and internal leadership resulting in this kind of unique corporate attitude across the board with their people from their drivers to their corporate boardroom. I truly wish I could give more companies this kind of endorsement but I do not give my name and reputation to anyone unless they have earned it! If you haven't tried FedEx, or used them recently, give them a try.

Questioning your lunch companion with this phase of your research should take only about 15 minutes. Do not allow phase one of your lunch to go beyond 15 to 20 minutes or you will run out of time for the second phase. Most business people consider their lunch hour to run from the time that they leave the office until the time that they return. Most employers follow that same time frame for their employees.

Be sure you use a restaurant close to the client's office so that you do not waste time driving to and from the restaurant. Also, be sure to tell your business friend that you will pick him or her up for lunch. Make certain that your car is immaculate inside and out. Ensure that everything in your car is clean, like files and briefcases, and neatly organized. Remember that you do not get a second chance at a first impression!

After your lunch has been served, ask your customer if they want dessert. Most will say, "No, thank you." Most business people do not eat dessert with lunch. Immediately ask the person waiting on you to bring you the check. Always use a credit card, preferably American Express, because it always puts you in the business winner category. Never pay cash unless you have no choice! It makes other people uncomfortable and they often feel like they should offer to pay half of the bill or at least leave the tip. If you must pay cash, excuse yourself, take the bill with you to the washroom and pay it on your way back. Always give 15% or more for the tip. Successful business people notice things like this and they like to do business with people who know "the rules." If, for any reason, you cannot do the math in your head, because you are nervous or just not good at math, try this technique. Compute 10% of the bill, which is easy math, and just double it. Even on a fairly large bill, it is only an extra dollar or so difference and it will get you past a normally uncomfortable moment, with style! Once the bill is paid, put your credit card and receipt away. Now you do not have to waste valuable time trying to get your waitress or waiter's attention or stand in line to pay the bill when the lunch crowd is coming in. Remember, every minute counts!

Save the last five minutes of your lunch meeting to close up the interview. Say this, "(client's first name), thank you so much for helping me and for being my friend!" Sincere appreciation and recognition of the people who have helped you is the first step of Selling From The Heart.

Unless you did not follow these steps correctly, you will feel a genuine sense of friendship in return from your client. If they did not want to help you, they would not have accepted your lunch invitation. After all, they know you want something because everyone knows, "There ain't no free lunch!"

On your way back to their office, keep your conversation light and friendly. Do not thank them again. You have already thanked them once. After you drop them off at the front door of their office or wherever they ask to be dropped off, pull away and park where they cannot see you.

Pull out their 5x7 client card and record all of the personal information you learned from your lunch meeting. Record their birth date, the names of their family members, friends, co-workers, and any other important information you can recall. You will be amazed and delighted to witness how fast you can build a professional relationship with someone when you are able to refer to their family, friends, co-workers, and other information from your conversations. Everyone enjoys working with people who take the time and make the effort to remember him or her and what he or she said. You will also endear yourself to your clients more by asking about the people, places, and things that they are interested in than almost any other thing you can do or say. If you happened to pick up an anniversary date, send your client a congratulations note one week before their anniversary. I have had wonderful results doing this with clients.

Next, open your glove box and pull out the appropriate Image Transfer System note and envelope, and address the envelope with the "magic" pen. "What is Image Transfer System," you ask? Well, I'm glad you asked, because that is the next chapter.

Keep reading, you are going to love this!

CHAPTER FOUR
THE IMAGE TRANSFER SYSTEM

THE ULTIMATE SYSTEM FOR BUILDING PROFESSIONAL RELATIONSHIPS

Early on in my quarter century of sales I learned the value of sending handwritten acknowledgement notes. For a couple of years I fell victim to the BELIEF that my written correspondence needed to be typed. I noticed, however, that the power behind handwritten notes got me remembered. I also noticed which of my incoming correspondence got my attention. I observed that almost everyone, including me, sorts his or her mail in three piles. I call the first of these piles the "A" stack. That is the "Always makes me feel good" stack. It is not only your smallest stack of mail, it is your most desirable stack of mail. This is the pile where you get handwritten notes, cards, and letters that you always open first.

I noticed that I often open my "A" correspondence on the way back from the mailbox. Most people I have talked to agree that they, too, open their "A" mail right away. Imagine the benefit to your personal, professional, and economic lives if all of your correspondence reached the "A" pile.

Next, is the "B" pile. This is the stack of "Bills" and other "stuff" with which we must deal. We all know that we need to open this stack of mail but we do not have the same positive frame of mind as we do with the "A" pile mail.

The third, I call the "T" pile. That is the one closest to the "Trash" into which we put all of the junk mail if we are not interested enough to open it or we don't have time to open it. Most people, including me, sort the "T" pile mail closest to the trash so that we can push it into the trash easily. It is really important that your correspondence never reach the "T" pile!

I have a long and successful history in direct mail marketing and lead generation. A large part of my success was from developing a **success system** to get the majority of my direct mail opened and read by my target audience. Remember this Steven Lloyd-ism.

> "*If you are experiencing a problem, you are lacking a **success system**. Convert your problem to a system and you no longer have a problem, you have a system! If the system stops working, change only one component part of the system until you gain or regain success!*"

These few sentences have done more to automate success for my clients and me than any other single thing I teach. Following it faithfully is where I come in as a coach!

Hopefully, by now you have already seen that this entire book is one grand **success system**. Please BELIEVE me when I say that everything I will ever teach you through my books, audiocassette tapes, films, or my live workshops is tested and proven to work at a very high success percentage. I practice what I teach everyday personally, professionally, and economically. I do not BELIEVE in nor do I teach "slap it against the wall and hope some of it sticks" mass marketing. I know what works. This knowing only comes from personal and up-to-date experience.

I know you have probably bought books and tapes and paid to attend expensive training programs only to find that what you learned does not work. Well, I was the guy "sitting next to you" in the seminar or "standing next to you" in the line to buy the tapes and books. I really do understand! I have spoken and trained professionally since 1981. I did not, however, write a book until now. Why? Because I was busy testing my ideas and concepts and proving them to be effective. I have developed them into powerful, results-driven **success systems** that are transferable to anyone who will study them and apply the principles. PDR (Practice, Drill, and Rehearse) these principles for 63 days (three 21-day cycles) so that they become a part of you. If you do, you will be amazed and delighted how well they will work for you too!

I am not trying to impress you with time and dollars, but I am trying to impress upon you that 100% of everything you read, listen to, or watch from me has thousands of hours and millions of dollars of testing. Most importantly, there are tens of millions of dollars of potential value for you! I say potential because the one unknown in this training is you.

Please understand that there are two reasons why education and motivation materials end up in garage sales next to the black velvet painting of the dogs playing cards. There is a very good reason why their original owner is willing to sell them for pennies on the dollar of their original price tag. The first reason is something to which we have already agreed. The content they are teaching is not tested and proven to produce consistent results. If it was, he would probably not accept any price for these materials if he could not replace them, true? Think about the value you place on systems, tools, and techniques that have proven to generate real value for you. I own out-of-print books and out-of-circulation tapes that have benefited my life tremendously. It would take a lot of money to buy these treasures from me.

The second reason is equally causative. The buyers of the materials do not read, study, learn, and apply what the materials teach. I have invested hundreds of thousands of dollars in seminars, books, and tapes. We have already agreed that many are significantly less worthwhile than they are represented to be. However, I have never bought even one book or tape or attended even one workshop where I did not get some value. Admittedly, I am and have always been a "sponge" that seeks out the most value and "drinks" it in. I have enjoyed a lifelong love affair with personal growth and development.

My goal in my work is to give such incredible value that the personal, professional, and economic lives of my students are improved beyond any measure of time or capital invested. What I am about to share with you will, if you follow the recipe to the letter, take your professional selling career and income into the next Dynamic Dimension. If you do what I teach you here, you will wonder why anyone would ever try to sell any other way!

I understand the salesperson mindset. I understand that you may want a shortcut into mastering the Image Transfer System. The Image Transfer System contains all of the tools and all of the training I am about to describe. I mention this only because many of my professional selling students and sales managers asked me to produce an all-in-one system so that they would not have to try to duplicate my recipe. (If you want to learn more, see the Resources Section in the back of this book).

So you will feel completely comfortable using this system, let me ask you this question: If you saw the value of and agreed to write 25 hand-written notes per week, would you agree that the notes would mostly fall into three or four basic categories? By categories I mean a "Nice talking to you or meeting you," a "Thanks for your time," a "Thanks for your business" category, and probably a "You are really a special friend for helping me so much" category.

Doesn't it seem reasonable that even if you were to create this system on a word processor, as many people do, that you could and would say pretty much the same thing to each recipient in each note or letter in a given group of business activities or interactions? Hopefully by now you are nodding your head up and down and saying, "Yes!"

I am sure of this categorization system because I have asked this same question to thousands of people. They all agree that they categorize their outgoing communications.

I even saw my daughter Jessica do this with her graduation thank you notes. "Thank you for your gift of money. I am putting it with my other money gifts and investing it in my college fund. Thanks so much for remembering me on my high school graduation," was one stack. She had another stack that said, "Thank you for your gift, I really loved it, you are so thoughtful!" There was another small stack that was custom written for the really nice gifts she received or notes to truly special people in her life.

I said, "Wow, a system!" Each person gets a handwritten note acknowledging him or her for what they have done or given!

What if it were possible for you to do the same thing but you only had to write the original master note once? Then the master is Image Transferred to special note cards that cannot be detected from handwritten. Then all you have to do is hand write the matching envelope with the same "magic" pen with which you wrote the master note with and attach a commemorative postage stamp.

What if I told you that I had personally tested this **success system** with thousands of people and not one person has ever asked me if it was a copy? It's true! This **success system** is so good that the Image Transfer note cannot be detected from the original master even under a magnifying glass!

For years I have taught the value of sending handwritten follow-up notes. Thousands of sales people have agreed with me that they have actually witnessed this process create major value. They even showed me large commission checks that came directly from those handwritten note card relationships. Why do the vast majority of salespeople stop doing what helped them to become so successful?

Over the years, I have asked thousands of salespeople who started sending original handwritten notes why they stopped. The overwhelming majority said, "It took too much time!" To hand write even a generic four-line note and envelope including name, address, and ZIP code, takes 2.47 minutes on average. This is not very much time until you consider that to build a large successful business using the personal direct mail strategy, you need to send approximately 100 notes per month! To the busy salesperson, four hours per month appears to be a lot of time.

Most new salespeople that are willing to hand write 100 notes a month in the beginning do so because they have little to do when they first start. As soon as the suspects-to-prospects and prospects-to-leads conversion process starts to bear fruit, the leads soon become clients. Clients require follow-up and service. Time becomes scarce. When you add the telephone follow-up and follow-through procedures required to make the **success system** produce the kind of results I claim it will, the average person will not follow a handwritten note marketing strategy consistently. The reason is because their pain of not having new clients is gone, and so is their spare time. Even when those very same salespeople saw the results in their own commission checks, they stopped. This is the CAUSE of sales slumps.

In my Managing From The Heart program, I have a secret system to teach sales managers to know if their salespeople stop using my automated **success system** that I am about to describe. I am not going to reveal it here because I do not want to spoil the future management value.

Most of us got into selling because it is a much easier form of earning a living than most of the other forms of labor. However, the economic prosperity and the relative ease of earning money can become your ally or your obstacle to World-Class results.

I was raised on a farm. Farming is a great laboratory to see the universal law of CAUSE and EFFECT work on a daily basis. Farmers cannot decide to not milk the cows or not clean the barns or not feed the stock for even one day. Even if they have more money in the bank than they need to pay the bills, they must do each step of their farming success formula. Even if they feel sorry for themselves that they have not had even one day off for 10 years (not uncommon), they must do each step, or failure starts to show its ugly head quickly! My farming background is what taught me to be so systematic in my thinking and actions.

The **success system** I am about to teach you is very much like farming. You can also rely on the *fact* that the "crop" I will show you how to plant will produce a bountiful harvest. Your role in this relationship is to continue to plant, cultivate, fertilize, water, and care for your "crop." You can and must trust the highest Power to provide the rest of what is needed.

Farmers who have completed every step of a successful planting do not race back to the machine shed and get their harvesting equipment.

Farmers know it will take between 100 and 120 days before the crop is ready to harvest. They also do not run out to the field every 10 days or so to dig up their plants to see if the roots are growing! They KNOW they are growing!

Your job is far more simple, less expensive, and far less labor intensive. Yet your farm will produce your first crop in 30 days or less and generate much more profit! Herein lies the challenge. Like a good farmer you must harvest and keep planting. If you do not, you will not have a second crop! By my observation, most salespeople, even veterans of our profession, restart their career two to four times every year.

Remember the base law of the universe: CAUSE and EFFECT. Look at the following chart and see if you also see a pattern that could be your pattern. Remember this chart contains the results of thousands of salespeople!

Does this chart look familiar to you? If you are a sales manager, I know you are saying, "Yes!" If you said, "No" you are either one of the rare few who truly understands "farming" and you do all of the steps every day; or what is more likely, you have not charted your own personal production over a six-month to one-year period of time. Go back through your own sales records and chart your production. Look at the CAUSE of both your peaks and your valleys. The objective of this chapter and this chart is to show you the CAUSE of sales success and sales slumps and to show you what **you** can do to **never have another slump again!**

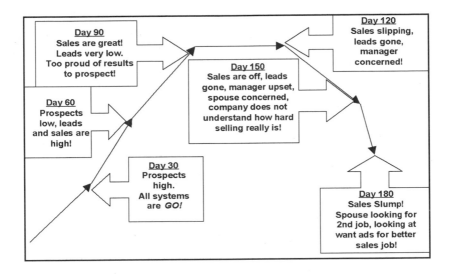

Stop deluding yourself that something or someone outside yourself is causing your sales slumps or holding you back in any way. That kind of thinking is the CAUSE that will put you on someone else's couch paying them $250 an hour so you can listen to yourself tell them about you! Look for the real CAUSE in every area of your life; put all of your time, talent, and resources toward changing it. You will turn the EFFECT around in 30 days or less if you focus on the CAUSE driving the effect!

Please notice I did **not** say your brain will necessarily enjoy what you see. I will not and cannot promise you a pain-free experience with this process for the first 21 days. According to Dr. Maxwell Maltz, the author of "*Psycho-Cybernetics*," it takes 21 days to **start** a new habit.

I have expanded Dr. Maltz's research. Personally, professionally, and economically, I have observed that it takes **three** 21-day cycles before you and your brain will adopt any new system. That's why I said earlier that you can have, and will have massive results with my **success system** in just 63 days. My most successful corporate clients bring me in to do live training and motivation every 2 to 3 months. They can measure the value of having me coach and encourage their salespeople and management teams to take the next 21-day step.

Live training and motivational education is very valuable if it supports ongoing and regular education. The most constantly successful sales organizations do both. They offer weekly sales and motivation education and bring live educators and motivation experts in to add that special live "spark" that only a live event can offer. Experiencing only live events without the consistent and ongoing education integration is what leads to the "motivation seminars don't last" BELIEF. You need **both** to build long term and lasting success!

So what do you do if you are self-employed or work for a company that does not offer this type of support for their people? What if you are the company and you cannot afford (yet) to bring me in personally? Because my mission—"Improve the way selling is done: From the Heart"— is for everyone, I created my books, audiocassettes and film series. You *can* afford that! In fact, I can prove to you that you cannot afford to be without it. If you will follow all of the steps I outline in my training, I guarantee that you will increase your sales income **five times the cost** of the training within 90 days or I will give you back all of your money! (If you want to learn more, see the Resources Section in the back of this book). And find out where my next *public* workshop is going to be and attend it. Each seat is very inexpensive. Or, look in your newspaper or on the Internet for any of the other World-Class trainers that will be in your local area and go to their program. You will gain a lot of the knowledge you need from them too! Or, you can continue to go up and down the sales chart. It really is up to you.

You can **ABI (Always Be Improving)**. You really can! There is not anyone or anything outside of you working against you. There is also **nothing** wrong with you! What you are experiencing is fixable, permanently! However, you must know and consistently do what the top performers know and do, consistently. If you learn and do what they know and do, you will have what they have! It is just that simple. This is not rocket science. It is also not hard work compared to farming.

My objective with each of my students is for them to dominate their sales chart. What does dominate your sales chart mean? It means that you ascend to and remain in the top 20% of your industry! Now, please do not give me all of the "why you cannot be there" excuses. None of them are valid. Your firm hired you and gave you a full commission because they BELIEVE in you. You have been given the same 100% chance that the top 20% performers have been given.

This is one of the many reasons I love professional selling so much. It is 100% fair, to 100% of all the salespeople, 100% of the time! If you do what the top performers do 100% of the time, you will have 100% of their results, 100% of the time. That is my recipe for success, and it really works!

Does that mean you will beat out the top performers for the number one spot? Not necessarily, top achievers are always very competitive. When you are on the top, stay humble. When you are on the bottom, stay encouraged! If you are lucky enough to get a true pro to take you under his or her "wing," always give him or her the credit for your success. If you do, they will keep helping you.

If you find yourself making excuses for your performance or feeling sorry for yourself, you need to know that 20% of the sales force in this world does not care about your problems or reasons for not being on the top. The other 80% are actually glad to see someone more miserable and less successful than they are! If you do everything, *and I mean everything,* that the top 20% do, you will enjoy what the top 20% have!

This is a perfect example of the law of CAUSE and EFFECT in action. I will say this one more time, so take it in. You **can** and **must** get into the top 20% club! If you do it for no other reason than economic reasons, just do the math. Look at the sales production numbers of the top 20% of the salespeople in your industry. Multiply your sales commission percentage times their sales production. Now, subtract your income. Big difference isn't it? Look carefully at what it is costing you to wait. Next year you will be one year older. Wouldn't you like to be earning what the top 20% in your industry earn? You **can** in less than one year!

Now I will show you all of the steps to automate the Image Transfer System. There are several specific component parts to make this **success system** work effectively for you. Please do yourself a favor and get **exactly** what you are instructed to get and do **not** cut corners or try to save a few pennies. You will be very glad you followed this success recipe when you see the results.

<u>**Step 1**</u> *Call PaperDirect*, Inc. at 800-272-7377 or go to their web site at **www.paperdirect.com** and order their product catalog. I want you to get a catalog even if you order your postcards and matching envelopes on-line. The fastest way to get what you need is on-line.

Look at the different styles and find one that resonates with you. You need to order one box of postcards and two boxes of matching envelopes because there are 200 postcards per box and 100 envelopes per box. You need enough supplies to use my **success system** for two months. Remember to mark your calendar two weeks out to reorder more supplies.

Most of the professionals I coach buy four months of supplies at a time. You can start with two months and a promise to reorder within two weeks from the date of your first order. I have worked with PaperDirect, Inc. for many years. They are professional and excellent to work with.

They occasionally have product on back order. That is another good reason to order your supplies in advance. In all of the time that I have worked with PaperDirect, they have never been out of product for more than a few weeks. However, if they are out of your product when you reorder, the entire **success system** is "off line" until you get more supplies. If you own a computer and printer with a CD-ROM drive, also order their template CD so you can have your card style on your computer. I will explain why later.

As you consider your card style, unless you intend to build an entire image theme around a particular style, I strongly recommend that you order one of their plain, no picture styles. Unless you are going to use the matching letterhead, envelope, folders, etc., you will create a better impression with plain cards and envelopes.

<u>**Step 2**</u> *Office Supply Store*. You need to get and order the following items: bright white ink-jet paper. This is the really good stuff for creating masters.

I recommend that you use Hammermill Jet Print Ultra. It is expensive per sheet, but you will only use it for the master templates for the Image Transfer System.

While you are at the office supply store, pick up a box of small binder clips. Get the smallest binder clips you can get. You will use these clips to hold your ITSN (Image Transfer System Note) master to your line master while you are writing your master note sheet. These clips really help keep the sheets aligned properly.

You can order your self-inking name stamp or personal adhesive address labels from the same store. The self-inking stamp or address labels should be ordered exactly as follows:

- Script print that is easy to read
- Your name on the first line
- Your mailing address on the next lines
- Dark blue ink if available

Here is what mine looks like.

Steven Lloyd
4121 Cross Bend Drive
Arlington, Texas 76016

The objective of your return address is to make the print as friendly and **personal** as possible. If you have or prefer to use professionally printed **personal** labels, they will work just as well and in some cases better. Just be sure that whichever return name and address method you choose appears personal and not from a business. That is why you should **not** use a P.O. Box or office address unless you are required by your management to use the company address.

If your company requires that you use the company name and address in business correspondence, it will not be as effective. As soon as you have the entire system put together, then and only then take it to your manager for approval, if you are required to do so. Just do **not** ask for permission until you are ready to show your manager the *entire* **success system** in its complete form.

To date, I have not had any of my students, who have followed my instructions to the letter, have their management stop them from using the ITSN (Image Transfer System Note) **success system**. In fact, quite the opposite is true. Sales managers really appreciate my **success system** and often adopt it for the entire office and many times pay for all or part of the cost.

You also need to purchase a 12-inch clear or see-through ruler, one box of thick rubber bands, one ream of regular 8½ x 11 photo copy paper, one Flair black ink writing pen and one box of Microball black Rollerball pens with 0.2mm point size. This is the "magic" pen I have been referring to. It is a critical part of the Image Transfer System.

Sanford Uni-ball manufactures these pens. It is imperative that you buy **black ink** only. It was the first pen of their line and is all black in color and thin in design. This pen is so important to your ITSN success that I have inventoried thousands of them to make sure my students have an endless supply.

Step 3 *Post Office*

Your next step is at the United States Post Office. Your objective is to buy four different commemorative postage stamps. Each quarter or so the United States Postal Service (USPS) offers a new commemorative stamp. You will need a minimum of 104 for the first month. That is 26 of each stamp. It is very important that you have four different stamps. Look at what is available to you and buy the ones that **you** like, but make sure that you have at least 26 of each of the four stamps.

Now you have a few days to prepare yourself while your component parts of this **success system** are on the way to you. I highly recommend that you pay for overnight shipping from PaperDirect. Remember that every day you are not using this **success system**, you have lost another day of planting time.

Step 4 *Locate A 300 dpi Copy Machine*

You now need to locate a photo-quality copy machine. This machine needs to have a dpi rating of 300 or higher.

When I designed this **success system** in 1989 I used Kinko's because they offer photo grade machines behind their counter. Today, most home office machines are rated 300 dpi rated or higher. The PaperDirect, Inc. products are designed to be used in copy, jet ink, and laser machines.

It will not hurt the machine. However, if you are planning to use a machine that you do not own, be sure to get permission to use it.

Step 5 *Go To The Grocery Store*

Next, go to the grocery store and buy a bottle of rubbing alcohol, a spray bottle, and a roll of paper towels. The rubbing alcohol is to be poured into the spray bottle and used to clean the glass of the copy machine each time you use it. Do not use regular glass cleaner. It has other "stuff" like ammonia in it that could damage the copy machine. Rubbing alcohol is very inexpensive, works great, and dries in seconds.

Step 6 *Clean The Glass*

If you look at the copy machine glass you will see why you need to clean it. Most machines that are 30 days old or older have fingerprints, smudge marks, white out, and other "stuff" all over the glass. Take the bottle filled with the rubbing alcohol and spray it directly on the glass of the copy machine. Take two paper towels folded into one to double the thickness and rub the glass briskly until it is dry. If the glass or copy area is excessively dirty you may need to repeat this process.

You will earn points with your management when they see you cleaning the glass on the copy machine. Do not try to clean the pad that touches the glass when you close the copy machine lid. Even though it may have marks on it from people holding open point ink pens in their hands, you will make it worse than it is by trying to clean it. The ink marks on the white pad will not affect your copy.

It is very important that you clean the glass **each time** you Image Transfer. If there is a scratch on the glass it will show up as a streak or a smudge on your Image Transfer copy. This **cannot** be fixed with rubbing alcohol. It most likely cannot be fixed without replacing the glass. If your reproduction continues to look imperfect, seek out and use another machine.

Step 7 *You Are Ready To Begin*

Well, now that you have all of your supplies, you are ready to begin. Be sure to run a test page by using a piece of regular copy paper to see that the Image Transfer System is coming through perfect on your machine. The way to accomplish this is as follows:

1. Take a clean sheet of master jet ink paper and lay it where your original master will be positioned on the clean glass.

2. Run a sheet of clean white regular copy paper through a copy cycle and look carefully at the copy. If you followed the glass cleaning instructions carefully and your reproduction is not coming through clean, find a different machine.

3. It is **critical** that you use a machine that is in the acceptable range for both **toner and drum service**. Your glass might be

perfect and you can still have dark streaks because of low toner or need for service of the drum.

The quality of the machine is so critical to this process that many of my students have gone out and purchased their own 300-dpi machine. They use it almost exclusively for my ITSN **success system**. If you are considering it, I recommend that you look into buying one of the Hewlett Packard OfficeJet "all-in-one" color jet ink systems. I use this system personally and it is wonderful. You can copy, scan, fax, and full color print with one system. The black Image Transfer System reproductions are also produced with ink and not dry toner. Stop at your office supply store with both your card stock and the ITSN master and try the HP Office- Jet. It really is amazing!

Remember that your Image Transfer System reproductions are only as good as the quality of the machine from which they come. Most well-maintained 300-dpi or higher machines will work just fine.

Please use the following checklist to make sure that you have everything you need to make this system function as designed.

---

1 PaperDirect catalog

1 box of Micro Rollerball Pens 0.2mm (Black Ink)

1 box of 4-up PaperDirect plain postcards = 200 cards

2 boxes of matching PaperDirect postcard envelopes = 200 envelopes

1 box of Hammermill Ultra jet ink bright white paper

1 clear plastic or see-through 12" ruler

1 Flair black ink writing pen to draw line masters

4 different commemorative postage stamps totaling 104

1 bottle of rubbing alcohol with spray bottle

1 roll of paper towels

1 300-dpi or higher copy machine access

1 self-inking name-stamp or personal return address labels

1 box of small binder clips

1 list of 250 prospects

1 ream of regular 8 1/2 x 11 photo copy paper

1 box of thick rubber bands

1 hour free of interruptions

Are you all set? Do you have everything? If you do not, please STOP and go get **everything** before you read any farther. Get everything you need, then proceed.

My goal is for you and I to develop a professional coaching relationship. I want you to have a 100% success result. For you to get a 100% success result, you must follow 100% of my instructions successfully. If you do not, you will have just another book sitting on your shelf; nothing will change. You will not get the desired result. You will not win and neither will I. Neither will I? How can I lose, you already bought my book? Think back to what I told you my desired result is where you are concerned. Do you remember? I need you to reach and maintain sales team dominance by getting into and staying in the top 20% of your industry.

I will settle for the top 20% of your office or your company for the first 90 days, but you need to know that my desired success result as your coach is for you to be in the top 20% of the sales force of your entire **industry**. This applies to everyone who says they are serious about success. Rookie or veteran, within one year I fully expect you to be in the top 20% of your industry! **Notice I did not say your office or your company, I said your _industry_!** By reaching the top 20% of your industry, you will automatically move to the top 10% of your company. Take your focus off the production charts in your office. Put your focus on your industry's success standard and you will see that it is relatively simple to become the number one sales producer in your office. Being ranked near the top of a production chart with other salespeople who are having a hard time paying their bills is not success, is it? Here is another Steven Lloyd-ism.

> *"If you always compete with the best, you will always experience the best from yourself!"*

You **can, must,** and **will** get into and stay in your industry's top 20% ranks. When you do, you will see for yourself that you will almost always be in the top 10% of your office or your entire company. You read about people all the time that found a **success system** and rose to the top of their industry in just one year. We have no time to waste because we only have 364 more days to get you there.

Your next step is to write your first set of Image Transfer System notes. You only need to write three; the fourth one will be blank. The reason for the blank card is simple. There are always certain situations that arise where writing a quick specific note is called for. Also, I like to send true handwritten originals every fourth or fifth time so the clients do not catch on to the system.

The next step is critically important and you will need an hour of uninterrupted time. No meetings, no incoming or outgoing telephone calls, nothing but focusing on this **success system**. If you do not have that hour now, please STOP reading until you do.

The first step to important business writing is to **think**. Think about the system you will be using. Let me suggest that your first card be what I like to call a "warm-up card." This is where you send an Image Transfer System Note to someone you want to "warm-up" before you call. I used this very technique to open a pathway to the chairman of the board of one of the largest American corporations. These people do not take calls from salespeople, yet, following exactly the same system that I will share with you, I was successful at getting a personal interview.

A personal story might help you see both the power of this system and how you may use it. Because some of the people who helped me along the way might feel uncomfortable with me using their names, I have changed the company name and the names of the individuals to protect them and my relationship with them.

I wanted to prove that I could get in to see a major international corporate player using my **success system**. I had a few contacts at Big Company International so I chose Mr. Robert Smith, Chairman of the Board. Mr. Smith has since retired but at that time he was almost as hard to see as the President of the United States. They provided him a Jet Ranger helicopter for his travel needs.

Here is exactly what I did and what you can do too. I called Big Company International Headquarters in Los Angeles, California. When the general receptionist answered I introduced myself and asked for the name of Mr. Smith's Executive Assistant. I was told her name was Rose. I said, "Thank you, please put me through to Rose's office." Much to my surprise, the next thing I heard was "Robert Smith's office." I was stunned how easy it was. They put me right through! I collected my thoughts, quickly regained my composure and said, "Is this Rose?" A smile came over her voice and she replied, "Yes, who is this?" I said, "This is Steven, (I paused) Steven Lloyd." This is when and where I learned one of the truly great secrets in "Dialing For Dollars."

My pause was accidental but exceptionally powerful. In my nervousness and the stammer of my own name, it came across as if she should know me. Being the real pro that Rose is, she came back with, "Hello Mr. Lloyd, how are you?" As I responded, I could hear Rose flipping through a card file. I found out later that this is exactly what she was doing. Rose asked me an open-ended question that could not be answered with a "yes" or a "no." It gave her a few seconds to flip through her card file to the "L" section and check for my name. I responded with, "I am very good today, I was wondering if you could help me?"

As I regained my composure, I was able to anticipate her next professionally trained response, which normally is, "How may I help you?" Most great gatekeepers use that phrase as a polite way of asking what you want so they can politely get rid of you and protect their boss. That is one of the main reasons they are there! Screening callers is a big part of their job and they all know it!

By leading her into what she was ready to say anyway, I felt a genuine sense of rapport and I could still hear the smile in her voice. In a small way it was like verbal dancing and she liked my lead. I said, "I have a personal note I need to send to Mr. Smith and I want him to open it personally. When would you suggest I mail it so he gets it?" She whispered, "If I were you, I would send it so it arrives next Wednesday." I said, "Thank you Rose. I will do just that and I will treat this as confidential information." Guess what she said to me? "Thank you." She thanked me! I said, "You're welcome, goodbye," and hung up.

That was the day another Steven Lloyd-ism was born.

"When you find yourself in a vein of solid gold, KEEP DIGGING!"

I wrote out the entire conversation and everything that I could remember about it. I will share all of the secrets I have discovered with **you**.

I sent Rose a thank you note for taking the time to help me. I also enclosed a 2" x 4" wonderful picture of a rosebud just opening, covered by droplets of morning dew. I said very sincerely in my note, "My brief conversation with you today gave me the same feeling on the telephone as looking at this rose picture, so I wanted you to have it!" Sincerity is a *golden key* that unlocks the door to the Heart. When I called again, do you think she remembered me? Please know that there is no replacement for genuine sincerity.

I sat down with a legal pad to pull my four-line Image Transfer Note together to Mr. Smith and here is what came out of 30 minutes worth of work.

> *Just a note to let you know that I have*
> *been a big fan of yours for several years.*
> *I would consider it an honor to interview you*
> *for my upcoming business training program.*
> *My <u>Best</u> Always,*
> *Steven Lloyd*

I Image Transferred that message onto card stock, hand wrote the envelope with the "magic" pen and wrote <u>*Personal*</u> at an angle in front of his name. When you send an Image Transfer System Note to a business contact, I suggest you only use their name, address, and ZIP code on the envelope. Again, I suggest that you always write the word <u>*Personal*</u> at an angle in front of the addressee's name so it catches the attention of the reader's eye and the eye of their gatekeeper. I put a commemorative postage stamp on the envelope (see the following example), and put the envelope with my other outbound mail.

I called my local post office and asked how long a first class letter should take from Irvine, California to Los Angeles, California. I was told it would take two days. I mailed it on Monday in case Big Company International had an internal mail system requirement of an extra day.

I called Rose on Wednesday as planned. I introduced myself again. It felt like I was talking to a friend. I asked if the card had arrived and I started to describe it. She said, "I put it on his chair personally and he mentioned it to me this morning." I asked, "Would you see if you can set me a fifteen minute appointment for anytime that he will see me?" She said, "Can you hold on?" I said, "SURE!" She was gone for several minutes. When she came back on the line she sounded excited saying, "Steven, can you be here at 10:00 a.m. tomorrow?" I said, "You bet I can!"

I drove up to Los Angeles two hours early, parked, found the executive tower, and went in to register. As the World-Class Executive Assistant she is, Rose had already called the security desk and had a security badge waiting for me.

If you have never gone through a security clearance for a high tech government contractor, you have no idea what you will experience. I thought they were going to strip search me!

The security staff at Big Company International would not allow me to take my camera or tape recorder into the meeting. I really wanted to get a picture of myself with Mr. Smith and to record our interview. No such luck and no such exceptions!

I was escorted to Mr. Smith's wing and delivered to Rose's desk. She smiled at me all the way down the long hallway. Rose was a lovely lady, well dressed, and very professional. Guess what she had sitting in a little stand on her desk? The picture of the rosebud I sent her!

She got me a cup of coffee and let Mr. Smith know I was there early. She said, "He is working on something very important and it may take a while to get in to see him." I thanked her for her courtesy and asked if I could work on some notes so that I would not interrupt her work. She said, "It is nice to meet someone who understands business etiquette."

Employers do not like or appreciate someone taking up their employee's time with idle chitchat. Employees are not there as paid entertainers.

After about 10 or 15 minutes and very close to our appointed time, Rose's telephone buzzed and Rose looked at me and said, "Mr. Lloyd, you can go in now." My face must have given away my emotions because Rose smiled warmly and said, "You can relax, he is a very nice man." Those words were like a needed key that unlocked the emotional ball and chain I was dragging.

I opened his door and walked into a huge private office. Mr. Smith was seated at his desk at the far right end of the room. I let go of the majority of my fear and decided to treat this like all of the other thousands of professional sales calls I had made. After all, the reason for the call was over. I had already won. I was in Robert Smith's private office! As I was closing the door, he looked up from his desk and said, "Hello young man, come in." He got up from behind his desk and walked half the distance between us to shake my hand. As soon as we shook hands all fear and discomfort left me. Mr. Smith has that rare ability to make you feel comfortable as soon as you meet him.

We were only supposed to have 15 minutes, he gave me over an hour! All I really did was ask him open-ended questions as I described in chapter three. Mr. Smith is no different than you or me. He enjoyed talking about himself to someone who was truly interested in what he had to say.

That was the day I learned that although it is harder to get to see the man or woman at the top, the higher you go the nicer the people are.

Mr. Smith did not get to be Chairman of the Board of one of the largest and most powerful companies in the world by being lucky. He got there and stayed there for many years. He survived through some of the toughest times in Big Company's history, by being **excellent** in every area of his life!

Hopefully this story demonstrates that this **success system** will work for you too. Also, I hope you noticed that **effort** is still required to get the appointments you want and need.

If you will follow my **success system**, you will soon see that you will be having interviews with people that you never dreamed possible. Now, let's design your Image Transfer System Note masters.

You can do this any way you wish. Here is another Steven Lloyd-ism I want you to remember.

" *You cannot do this wrong, only better!* "

You will find that you will change your Image Transfer System Notes from time to time. That is the way the system is designed to evolve. So let's proceed from the point of view that you have a list of 250 prospects. If you have done your suspecting research, you know the correct name of the key person and the correct address. You have also verified the telephone number because you did as instructed and called to verify the critical information. Now we will write a warm-up note.

Remember that this warm-up note goes on a piece of 8½ x 11 **regular** photocopy paper. Once you have designed and done your practice run on regular copy paper, you are ready to hand write the same notes on the expensive jet ink bright white paper. This second draft will be your master note sheet. The following example is one I use.

> *Just a note to let you know I will be calling you to discuss an idea that will dramatically increase your sales that I know you will find interesting. Please expect my call in the next few days.*
> *My Best Always,*
> *Steven Lloyd*

Here is why this particular ITSN (Image Transfer System Note) is so effective. First I give my prospect no information to object to or to reject. He or she has no way to categorize me. They cannot tell their assistant to shuffle me off to someone else because they do not know what I want! I also said I want to discuss an **idea** that will dramatically **increase your sales** that I know you will find interesting. My warm-up note cards are sent to the person who is responsible for doing what? Increasing sales! You will need to modify these words to fit your products and or services. Always remember that the person that you are trying to get in to see really needs what you sell. He or she just doesn't know it yet.

Most managers today have invested thousands of dollars into training that has convinced them that one single **idea** could be a major turning point in their career. Ideas are held in high esteem in the corporate world at all levels. What is the first question that a manager asks his or her staff in a crisis? "Who has an **idea** to solve this problem?"

Next, I have resolved my "getting through" issue with their gatekeeper. In my Image Transfer System Note I said, "Please expect my call in the next few days."

Check with your local post office for your first class delivery dates. I mail my cards on Wednesday for long distance delivery, Thursday for regional delivery, and Friday for city delivery. Why? So that all of my notes get to the desired destination by Tuesday or Wednesday of the next week, on average. The majority arrives on Tuesday, and a small percentage arrives by Wednesday. There will always be the situation where your piece of mail was either not delivered until Wednesday or later, or the person you sent it to did not receive it or open it at all. You cannot, however, design a system around single digit percentages.

Now, when you call and your target manager's gatekeeper answers, here is what you say. When the assistant says, "Hello," introduce yourself by name only and ask for the manager by name adding, "He or she is expecting my call." Remember, in your Image Transfer System warm-up note you told the target decision-maker to, "**expect my call.**" Normally the gatekeeper will put you right through.

There are only four options that can happen at this particular point:

1. They are not in or not available.
2. They will not take your call or you get screened.
3. You get their voice mail.
4. They take your call.

Let's take each of these possibilities one at a time.

1. *They are not in or not available.*

If you are talking to a live person, simply ask when the best time to reach (manager's name) directly is. There are only two options that can happen at that point:

• *You are asked for more information.*

In this case, simply say, "I sent (manager's name) a **personal** note and I would like to discuss it with (manager's name) **personally.** What is the best time for me to reach him or her personally?"

This will normally take care of the typical inquisitive gatekeeper. Remember that the gatekeeper has been trained to get the information he or she wants from ineffective salespeople who normally open up like a "ripe melon" with just one question. Because these salespeople have not been trained how to get past the gatekeeper, they normally get screened with just one question! Gatekeepers respond to authority. Remember that they report to a person who speaks in directives. If you answer their questions briefly and come back with an authority-based question like, "Will you put me through please?" They normally respond robotically the way you want them to because they are programmed to respond to positive authority.

- *You are told when to reach the manager directly.*

Simply make note of it and move on to your next call. As long as you know when to call him or her that is all you need to know for now.

2. *They will not take your call or you get screened*

Rarely will someone tell you that his or her boss will not take your call. They will normally give you some excuse or reason why they are not available. Simply continue to associate the reason for your call to your **personal** note and ask for a time of availability. Persistence is the *golden key* that unlocks most gatekeeper doors. If you cannot get through ask for the boss's voice mail.

3. *You get their voice mail*

In today's busy and aggressive business climate, getting someone's voice mail is common. Here is specific Voice Mail Magic dialogue to use. Remember that most of the people that you will be calling are looking for a reason to **not** take or return your call. Simply leave a message like this; "Hi (manager's name) this is (your name) and I'm calling to see if you got my card. Please call my private telephone number at (give area code first plus your seven digit telephone number). It's important that I talk to you personally. I'll be waiting for your call." Hang up and dial the general telephone number again and talk to someone live. Question either the receptionist or someone in another department to determine when the person you are trying to reach arrives at the office and what the best time is for you to call back. Again, **pleasant persistence** is the *golden key* that unlocks most prospects' doors.

The person who must accept 100% responsibility for follow-up and follow-through is **you**. If you are going to sit by your telephone and wait for people to call you back, you will starve in professional selling! Here is another Steven Lloyd-ism.

> *"Salespeople who do not follow through raise skinny children!"*

You must train yourself to be persistent if you are going to be a life-long member of the top 20% club!

4. *They take your call.*

When you reach the target decision-maker, the first thing to do is build rapport. If you have a name to drop of someone who knows him or her, or a name that he or she should know, drop it like this:

"(Manager's name), **your friend** Bob Jones over at XYZ Company suggested I call you. I was able to help Bob and he thought that I should get your opinion too. I called to set a 15-minute **opinion interview** with you to discuss how I may be able to help you to both lighten your work-load, **and** increase your profits. When my presentation starts, I will start a 15 minute timer and when it "beeps" if there's nothing else you would like to know, I promise to leave as a friend and not take up any more of your valuable time. What is the most open time in your schedule to meet me for 15 minutes- mornings or afternoons?"

It is your responsibility to **Practice, Drill and Rehearse (PDR)** so you present yourself as confident and effective. If you start to stammer and stumble at this point you will most likely lose most executives. They will **not** let you PDR on them!

The objective in this chapter is to design your follow-up notes. We will get to that next but remember that only one of four things can happen when you talk to the decision-maker:

1. He or she sets the appointment.

2. He or she puts you off to another time.

3. He or she stalls you with an excuse.

4. He or she declines your request.

If you study, learn, and **PDR** the ideas, strategies, techniques, and **success systems** I outline for you in this book, the fourth of the above four options will happen very seldom. If it does, just smile, shake it off, and move on to your next lead call.

You can use two or more notes for option number one of the above scenarios. The first note card should be sent thanking him or her for taking the time to see you. I like to use the following type of note to confirm option number one:

> *Just a note to say thanks for taking*
> *15 minutes out of your busy schedule*
> *for me. I know you will be glad you did!*
> *I look forward to our meeting.*
> *My <u>Best</u> Always,*
> *Steven Lloyd*

Here is the reminder note, the second note example for option number one, the successfully set appointment. The reminder note needs to be handwritten because of the different time and date required to make it effective. I use one that looks something like this:

> *Just a note to remind you of our upcoming*
> *meeting next Tuesday at 10 AM. I look*
> *forward to meeting you personally!*
> *My <u>Best</u> Always,*
> *Steven Lloyd*

Use whatever salutation you like. I have experimented with several over the years and found that "My <u>**Best**</u> Always" has proven to be the <u>best</u> for me. It resonates with my professional Mission. I am letting the reader know that I am willing to continue to give my <u>best</u>! Remember that every word that you use and the way you use it counts! Use whatever salutation you like. Just do not use one that could be questionable or create a negative impression with the person you are trying to reach.

Remember this Steven Lloyd-ism.

"*When you try to make an impression on another person, that is the impression you make!*"

Salutations like, "Passionately yours" sound nice. They are powerful and I have used them. Fortunately, I had several good friends who had the courage to tell me that it made them uncomfortable or rubbed them the wrong way. After all, isn't it up to your client to determine if you are passionate, successful, or powerful, at least as far as **they** are concerned? Be careful that your salutation does not reek of or can be perceived of as ego by telling someone that you are passionate, successful, or powerful. Consider a salutation that says what you are willing to do and not what you are. So, think carefully about the **last** impression that you want to leave with your correspondence. You don't get a second chance at a first or last impression. Until you are completely sure of your salutation you might want to stay with a time-tested, proven winner like, "Sincerely yours." Remember, every word counts!

Call your local post office to find out what the delivery time is to each ZIP code to which you are mailing first class mail. If you have at least two post office days and your meeting is **not** scheduled for early morning, get the "meeting reminder" note card to your prospect in the mail immediately. If you do not have time to send a reminder note, you need to confirm any appointment over 24 hours ahead of time by telephone, preferably with your prospect's assistant or their voice mail.

You can accomplish successful reminder messages without running the risk of talking directly to your prospect—which gives them the chance to cancel—by simply calling during a time of the day when they are most likely **not** going to take your call personally. Early mornings before 8:00 a.m., during lunch hour, or after 8:00 p.m., are your best times. Simply leave a message saying:

"(Manager's name), this is (your name) and I'm calling to remind you of our meeting at 10:00 a.m. tomorrow. I'm really looking forward to meeting you in person!"

Do not go on and on in your message. Being brief is the *golden key* that locks down the appointment.

Following your meeting, you will also need an ITSN card that says something like this:

> *Just a note to say thanks for seeing*
> *me and for the extra time you invested*
> *with me. I will follow up next week on*
> *the ideas that we discussed.*
> *My Best Always,*
> *Steven Lloyd*

If you will follow my **success system** to the letter, they will almost always invite you to stay beyond the promised 15 minutes. Remember that the promise was for a 15-minute presentation.

You might find the following note helpful for the second and third options.

> *Just a note to let you know that I have been try-*
> *ing to reach you personally. I have something*
> *important to discuss with you. I will call again*
> *next week. Please take my call, I know you will*
> *be glad you did!*
> *My Best Always,*
> *Steven Lloyd*

Now you have your three Image Transfer System Notes for your first master set. Remember that you need to leave the fourth one blank so that you have the opportunity to pen a note when needed and, it will be needed! Write whatever three, four, or five line message you want to use and have someone check your spelling and grammar. Remember that what you write is permanent! If you have access to a word processor with spell and grammar check, use that tool as well.

The next step is to create your line master template. If you have PaperDirect, Inc.'s software showing the post cards you bought, great. Call it up on your computer and save it as a file called "Post card lines." Now, double space (two returns) then use your **underline key** and type a line two returns from the top, all the way across the card. Again, double space (two returns) and repeat the process until you have seven double spaced lines providing seven spaces for writing, using the bottom line and spaces for your salutation and signature. Go up to your control panel on your PC and find the icon called, "Lines." Somewhere on your system you will find an option showing pre-designed lines of different thickness. Click, drag, and highlight the lines that you have typed. Next, click on the thickest line from your line menu box. It needs to be as thick and black as if you drew it with a **black** Flair, writing pen. If you do not have access to a computer, that is why you bought a "clear plastic see-through" ruler and a **black** Flair, writing pen. The lines should have approximately 1/2" distance between them. Use one of your four-card sheets to print or draw your lines on. Furthermore; if you are using the plain four-card stock I recommended that you buy, you need to draw a vertical line and a horizontal line on the perforation between your cards. This allows you to see the border of each card as you write your Image Transfer System Note master. This will be the line master for you to put under the piece of regular copy paper (test master page), then under your bright white Jet Ink paper (real master page).

Your next step is with a piece of **regular** copy paper. It is now time for you to write your notes on this **test** master page. If you want a perfect result, please follow these instructions to the letter!

Take two of the small clips you bought and clip your line master to your sample master sheet in the upper right-hand and lower left-handed corners. If you are left-handed, reverse this instruction.

Write only one note at a time and then take a three-to-five-minute break. You need to write all three of your notes with no errors. Once you have each of your three notes (up to seven lines, including the salutation and the signature) written on the test master page, you will know if your notes will fit on the real master page. If **any** of them do not fit, you must redo them until they do fit. Make a copy of the four-card sheet so you can run a test page on regular copy paper to be sure all the words fit within the borders. You will see if **all** of the words appear in the open areas without running onto the borders. If all the words do not fit perfectly, try again until they do.

Use only the Micro Rollerball, with **black ink** and 0.2mm size as outlined in your supply list. This is the "magic" pen. Once you have completed the test successfully, it is time to write your real master notes on the bright white Jet Ink paper. Once again, take a break between each of the three notes. Give your hand, eyes, and brain a brief rest. It is human nature to hurry when we write or to become momentarily distracted and make errors. If you make even a small mistake on any one of the three master notes, you must throw the entire master sheet away and start again. You will find, hopefully not the hard way, that taking a brief rest between each note makes all the difference in the world. If you do make a mistake, take a break before you start again. No one has their best penmanship skills available when they are nervous, tense, tired, or frustrated.

If you follow my instructions, you will see that you will complete all three notes on your first attempt. This **success system** was perfected by me making hundreds of mistakes to get to where we are today. You would not BELIEVE the supplies I threw away learning what I am teaching you now.

You have already completed your test run using the copy of the four-card stock and the handwritten test master note page. By now you should know how to place the handwritten master on the glass and what direction to feed your card stock into your machine. If you have **any** doubts about exactly how and where to place your master, run another test page on regular copy paper. Please do not waste expensive card stock. If all systems are "go," run **one** four-card sheet (your first), and look again at every detail. You will be amazed and delighted at how great they look! Go ahead, take a magnifying glass and look at it. You cannot tell it from the original handwritten master can you? I told you that you would love this **success system**! If you can tell a difference, you need to use a different machine.

Now, load 25 more four-card stock sheets in the machine's automatic paper feed tray. Because you have changed the paper stock from what the machine has been conditioned to use, I recommend that you run only **one** at a time from your 25 stack. If it prints perfectly, continue to press the "start" or "copy" button and check each one to be sure it is perfect. Your four-card stock is expensive and the "one at a time" process does not take much more time compared to doing them all over again because something went wrong with the Image Transfer process.

Now, take your **first** Image Transfer System four-card sheet and break it into four separate cards. You will find the following tip very helpful. Fold the 8½ x 11 sheet in half so that the top of the page touches the bottom and you break the perforation. Then fold it again in the opposite direction to break the perforation. You will notice that the per-foration breaks easily. Pull apart those two folds. Now repeat this process with the two remaining halves. Do **not** try to pull them apart without folding the sheet to break the perforation or you will tear at least one card. Trust me, I've done it!

You now have four separate note cards in front of you. Three have Imaged Transferred handwriting on them and one is blank. Take out your four **different** commemorative postage stamps, pull one stamp from each of the four **different** postage styles and place one of the **different** stamps on each of the **different** Image Transfer System Notes in the bottom left hand corner of the note card. This way you will always know which stack has the **different** note card in it, even when the note cards are placed in and sealed in the envelopes with the **matching** postage stamp attached. You will carry your "stamped samples" with you on top of the sealed, stamped envelope. The **different** postage stamp will always let you know which card you are sending.

Next, assign each one of your stamped samples a code like **1A, 2A, 3A,** and **4-blank** so you can mark your 5x7 client-cards. This way you will always know which card you sent. Set the note cards bearing the dif-ferent stamps on the top of your desk. Next, take 25 envelopes and place the correct postage stamp for that stack of Image Transfer System notes in the upper right corner of each of the 25 envelopes.

Now that you have finished posting those envelopes, take your new self-inking name stamp or address labels and return address the **back flap** of each of the 25 envelopes. It is an important part of the system for you to put your name and address on the **back flap** of each envelope. Take only one envelope at a time and carefully press your stamp impression or return label firmly on the back flap of each envelope. When you are fin-ished, put the note card with the matching postage stamp on the top of that stack of envelopes. Repeat this process with each of the other three remaining stacks. As soon as you have finished the envelopes, retrieve your stack of Image Transfer System printed cards from the copy machine.

Repeat the folding and breaking of the perforation and pulling apart process. Put the matching card into the matching envelope. To avoid any possibility of error, complete only one stack at a time. Then wet and seal each envelope, one stack at a time. Using rubber bands that will not break easily and yet are large enough to hold your stack without bending it, band each of your four stacks.

Now you are ready. I strongly recommend using only your Micro Rollerball "magic" pens for **everything** you do from now on. It is a great pen and you **never** want to run the risk of addressing an Image Transfer System Note card envelope with any pen except the same "magic" pen that you wrote the master note with.

Keep two of these "magic" pens in the glove box of your car with your "Thanks for your time" note cards. Remember that you **must** address the envelopes with the same pen. I've tried several different pens over the years of the development of this **success system. None** are more consistent than the one I have described. Again, be careful in your selection of the point size when you buy your pens. It must be the 0.2mm micro size. The pen I use is the first Micro Rollerball pen produced. It has the all black body with a silver-colored metal clip. I have tried dozens of different pens and this one is the only one that will give you the kind of results you need.

You do not need to know why it works, you only need to know that it works and what to do. Remember, that is why you "hired me" as your coach. Much like the pioneers of the old west who hired a guide, they were only concerned about having a safe, successful journey to the Promised Land. The guide's job, as is mine, is to get you there with the best possible results!

EMAIL MAGIC

Email is another way of reaching decision makers today. Email is a new and unique form of correspondence. In chapter eleven I will teach you about the three different brain languages. Email is visual-based communication and therefore activates or triggers most people's visual cortex. Most of the email messages I read are ineffective because they do not consider the following four critical factors:

- The subject line must be eye-catching.
- The body of the email must be brief.
- The email must get the reader to take action.
- The email must contain your contact information.

The subject line must be eye-catching and interesting. If it is not, you may not even get your email opened. Today, most business executives receive dozens of emails every day. Most follow the same procedure. They open the email index and look at the subject line. Next, they look at the "sender" line or address. They either open it or they don't. If they don't, it doesn't matter what you said, because they didn't read it. Think of the email subject line as a headline in a newspaper, magazine, or advertisement. If you will invest the time needed to write your subject lines like you would if you were investing thousands of dollars in advertising, you will see a remarkable difference in your email response results. I suggest you test these subject lines on other people before you send them to prospective clients. Try sending them to people on your sales team or in your family to get their input and reaction. I also suggest you send them to yourself so you can see them for yourself.

Here are a few sample subject lines that I use in promoting my books, tapes, films, and workshops. These will give you some successful examples to help you get started:

- Here is the answer that you have been looking for!
- Do you sell from the Heart?
- Here is the secret that will help you keep your job next year.
- Is your competition using this secret weapon against you?
- Please look at this and let me know what you think.

If they do open your email, you must make your point as briefly as you can without sacrificing quality. Try using what I call the one, two, one Email **Success System**. One subject line, two brief paragraphs, one action.

Your email needs to start with a quick, friendly statement explaining how you got their email address and why you are writing to them. Never spam! Spamming is where you have collected email addresses that were attached to another email you received. If you buy a list tell them "You are on a list of people who have indicated that you want to receive the latest information on (fill in what you do)." If you are "bulk" emailing always give them the opportunity to get off your list. Put the "to remove yourself from our information hotline list" hyperlink at the bottom of your email, **not** at the top.

Next, make a big promise that you know you can exceed. Remember that you need to get their attention and hold it. Email readers and web surfers think and react in microseconds. In broadcasting, my very first station manager Russell Brown said, "Steven, always remember that you are one 'click' from unemployment." What he meant was that you and I must keep the mind of our audience engaged all the time. I am doing everything I know to achieve this with you right now. If I don't keep your brain entertained you will simply stop reading. My job is easy compared to email success. You have already made an investment in my book. Email, however, is sent via a medium that requires major focus and testing to work. I get hundreds of emails per week and I have for many years. If you have used email for any length of time, you know what I mean. Very seldom do I receive an email that gets my attention, holds my interest, and causes me to take action. The reason is because email is a new medium compared to print, radio, or television. I was trained in radio. I learned quickly that when you have only the ear and auditory devices to use to get and hold the attention of the listener, you must use every tool in your box. Television is simple by comparison because you can use the visual and auditory areas of the brain to catch and hold the viewer's attention. With email and Internet marketing, you have only one to three seconds to get their attention. You have only seven seconds to build interest. You only have 28 seconds to get them to take action.

If you succeed at getting their attention, you have another three to five seconds to hold their attention for each point. Each sentence is a new point. Each point needs to be short and to the point. Most email minds cannot or will not continue to read on and on about a subject unless or until they find it interesting. Never buy into the BELIEF that, "They were not interested." Accept the truth and responsibility that, "I was not interesting!" If you correctly present your ideas, you can make any subject interesting.

The last but equally important goal of the business email is to get the reader to take action or for you to be remembered. Getting your prospect to take action can be something as simple as, "Print this page now so you will have my attached contact information to reach me later." If you use a web site to promote what you do or what you sell, you can include a hyperlink right in your email so your reader can just click on it and it will take them to the exact page you want them to look at. Remember that just because the hyperlink appears in blue (indicating that it is an active link) on your screen, it will transfer as a hyperlink to the screen of your prospect. Several internet service providers, such as America Online, are unlinking the hyperlink unless you are on their system. Many corporate servers are also programmed to do the same. So always add the sentence, "If this hyperlink does not appear in blue on your screen, simply click, drag, copy, and paste it into the web address line of your browser and press enter." This simple but important instruction will teach everyone how to reach your web site or web page. Remember that we are still many years from everyone knowing how to use what you might think are "the basics" of the Internet.

If you do not have a web site or your goal is only to have the person you are emailing remember you, you should still include an email signature line which includes your name, address, telephone number, fax number, and email address. Many people print emails that they want to look at or respond to later. If you have all the ways your prospect could possibly contact you on your email signature, they may indeed call or email you later using that contact information.

Each server system or ISP has different methods for setting up an email signature. If yours doesn't allow you to create a signature, you can still achieve this by creating one on a blank email. Then you can click, drag, and copy it into a word processing blank file. If you save the file as, "email signature" you can open it, click, drag, copy, and paste it into each email message before you send it. Once your signature contact information is in your "click, drag, and copy" cache memory, all you need to do is point your mouse pointer at each new blank email screen, click your right mouse button (for PC users), and select "paste" with each new message, and there is your signature! This is a very important step of Email Magic.

Following this Email Magic **success system** will improve your response dramatically. It will also help you to be remembered. The secret behind this **success system** is: always think about how you can help the person you are writing. We all want to listen to or read about things that will make our personal, professional, and economic lives better.

You are now ready to start the most amazing and meaningful of all journeys: **The journey into the Heart!**

CHAPTER FIVE

The Journey Into The Heart

THE MOST PRODUCTIVE TRIP YOU WILL EVER TAKE

The journey this time, oh pioneer friend of mine, is the best, most valuable journey you will ever take. It is the journey into the Heart! When I get you there, you will see bountiful Fields of Opportunity, vast Prairies of Possibility, and Mountains of Rewards. We do, however, need to cross the River of Skepticism, traverse through the Cavern of Salesperson Pain, and respectfully navigate the Graveyard of Dead Relationships.

Two Guards protect the Hearts of your prospective clients. On the left is the Warrior of Intellect. On the right is the Adviser of Emotion. Both will test you. If you pass both of the Guards, you will be permitted to enter the Kingdom of the Heart. If you fail either test, you will be sent away or stopped dead in your tracks and given no explanation for your lack of forward progress.

It is comparatively simple to pass the test of the Intellect by showing the mind that you are informed, organized, priced right, and dependable.

Simple training and education requirements that I will teach you will achieve the majority of the requirements of the Warrior of Intellect. It will also bring you a commensurate monetary reward. If that is truly your only goal in reading this life-long work of mine, keep reading because you will find tons of new, time and completely tested, results-oriented ideas, techniques, systems, and recipes for selling success.

Are you one who has grown tired of the "dog and pony show" type of selling? Do you BELIEVE that you are capable of going beyond the compensations that come from just entertaining the Warrior of Intellect to the point of reward? Well, you may be ready to move into and master the next level of true professional relationship building. I call it Heart Selling!

Heart Selling is not only more effective and CAUSES more monetary compensation, you will see that it is a new and rewarding way to truly live as well as sell.

If you will let go of your judgement, training, and BELIEFS about how selling is done, you will see the World-Class results for yourself. You will personally witness that your investment in this book and, more importantly, the time you are investing, has the real potential to bring you the true rewards that you have been seeking personally, professionally, and economically.

At some level, you already know that money and all of the wonderful things it buys are a short-term motivation. Is money really all that important? Yes, absolutely! I would be the last person to tell you that money and earning lots of it is not important. Money, however, will not truly satisfy you. It will only help you get your wants. It is however, only an EFFECT. Money cannot and will not satisfy your inner needs!

We are all guided, motivated, and supported by four basic human needs or CAUSE motivations. These needs are **control, security, approval, and acceptance**. Think of them as the four main foundational legs that support your entire BELIEF system.

When these needs are satisfied, you experience a state of being called happiness. When any one of these human needs are not met with the results you feel are necessary, that lack triggers a BELIEF that says, "I'm not okay."

Money will not truly satisfy any of these four needs. You may be saying, "Steven, that's why I bought your book, so I could learn how to earn lots and lots and lots of money!" Well, I have some great and not-so-great news for you. The great news is that if you follow all of the secrets and **success systems** exactly as I outline them in this book, you will earn lots and lots and lots more money. The not-so-great news is that you will still not have your inner needs for **control, security, approval,** and **acceptance** truly satisfied. Those important needs are only truly satisfied by living a life of purpose, giving, and helping other people get what they want and need. Earning lots and lots and lots of money, while you do that, is truly heaven on earth.

I know several millionaires. The vast majority of them "worshipped" money as if it was their God, BELIEVING that more is better. Well, more will never truly satisfy you.

I enjoy and appreciate everything my money has bought me. However, it is not the money or anything it buys that gives me my sense of **control, security, approval,** and **acceptance**.

I remember very clearly the day I looked at my tax returns and one of my advisers asked me how it felt to be a multimillionaire. I said, "It does not feel any different than when I made a good enough living so that I did not have to worry about how I was going to pay my bills!"

I grew up in the '50's. There was a popular TV show called THE MILLIONAIRE. The story line was about a wealthy gentleman who researched good and deserving people. He would have his assistant, Mr. Anthony, seek them out and deliver a tax-free check for one million dollars to one of the people he had selected. There was only one condition: the benefactor required that he stay anonymous.

Each episode gave you a roller coaster ride of joy, happiness, excitement, and relief. It also taught you that along with tremendous wealth comes some pain: the pain of responsibility, the pain of not knowing who your real friends are. Each week you would see, hear, and experience the same scenario acted out in unique and different ways. The writers of the show did a wonderful job showing the diversity of human culture as it relates to what we think we want.

The vast majority of us have our attention on what we do not have and we do not express appreciation and gratitude for what we do have. The philanthropist who gave away the money took great care to only give the one million dollars to people he was convinced would do no harm with it. Each week, almost without exception, the different recipients all came to the same conclusion. "It is not how much you have that matters; it is what you do to help others that CAUSES true wealth."

Living a life of purpose, giving, and helping other people get what they want and need is the golden key that unlocks the door to true **control, security, approval,** and **acceptance.** Having all these needs satisfied and in perfect balance brings a state of being called happiness!

Study for a moment one of the wealthiest people to ever live. This person lived where she wanted to live. She ate what she wanted to eat. She was even interviewed on Larry King Live! She traveled the Four Corners of the world. She saw the wonders of the world.

She was completely approved of from the most needy beggar in the street to Presidents and even the Pope! She had 100% security in every area of her life including physical, emotional, monetary, and spiritual.

She was in great demand worldwide and she commanded great wealth. When she needed millions of dollars for a project, all she needed to do was to direct that millions of dollars be given to a project and millions of dollars poured in. She was in complete control of her personal and professional lives as well. She controlled all of the circumstances around her that she could and those she could not control or change, she called on the highest Power in the universe and waited and watched patiently.

I do not BELIEVE that the thought of being promoted to the highest position in her organization ever crossed her mind. However, the Roman Catholic Church is considering Mother Teresa for sainthood!

I also BELIEVE that if Mother Teresa had chosen a path of service in business or industry she would have left an indelible mark there as well. Had she applied the same skills, dedication, commitment, determination, and faith in business, she would have built a worldwide economic empire equal to another one of my lifelong heroes, Sir John Templeton.

Do not judge someone else's life. Study how successful people accomplished what they did and apply the same success formulas through your own uniqueness. If you do, you will have a unique and special demonstration of what is possible for your life.

I put this chapter where it is in this book for a very important reason. I understand that if I am to help you create any real and lasting value in your life, I must be given passage into **your** Heart. I also know that your brain must see, hear, and experience my intellectual value before you are willing to even consider allowing me to have any emotional influence in your life.

For me to teach you the most powerful, useful, and valuable information of how to access someone's EBC (Emotional Buying Center), I must have access to yours.

We have now reached the first adventure in Selling From The Heart. For you to be given access to someone else's EBC, they must understand and BELIEVE that you will do them **no** harm.

To illustrate my point, see if you can find yourself in the following scenario. Have you ever been in a personal or business relationship where you completely admired, BELIEVED, and trusted someone? You were 100% convinced at all levels that they were trustworthy, and then you found out that you were wrong. How did you feel about this person when you found out that they were not worthy of your trust? How do you currently feel about this person today? Did you do or say anything to get even? Would you ever trust them again? Have you ever been guilty of causing someone else this kind of pain?

The emotion of pain comes from your Emotional Buying Center. In this work the word Heart is interchangeable with EBC. You can call it either one and still be correct. It does not really matter what you call it; however it is essential to understand how it works and how you can make it work for everyone's benefit. Recall the Steven Lloyd-ism.

> **"*T*he clearer your understanding is, the better your results are."**

Before we proceed, you need to know that what I am about to teach you has the power to create more benefits, control, and positive effects than anything you have ever used as a professional salesperson. It also has the power to work in the opposite direction if you misuse it.

With the advent and popularity of the World Wide Web, your reputation can and will be enhanced worldwide in a matter of months if you sufficiently, emotionally, and beneficially enhance enough other people's lives with what I teach you. It is not possible for you to yet appreciate the significance of this statement. Once you have studied, learned, practiced, drilled, and rehearsed (PDR) the techniques, skills, and **success systems** I teach in this book, you will see the results and power I describe. Positive change will happen for you faster than you ever dreamed possible!

Please BELIEVE me when I say that it is very important that you read, agree, date, and sign the following EBC commitment. Please do **not** proceed with your studies until you have put ink to paper and signed this agreement. If this is your book, date and sign the following agreement right here in this book. If you have borrowed this book, please copy this agreement to a separate piece of paper or into your notebook or journal and date and sign it there.

The EBC Commitment

I, the undersigned, understand the potential power, value, and responsibility of using the EBC techniques described in this book. I hereby agree to only use what I am about to learn to benefit **all** that they affect. I agree to never change someone's personal BELIEFS without being requested by him or her to do so.

I agree to only use my EBC skills, abilities, and techniques for the **good** of all parties concerned.

Date: _____

X _____
  Signature

CHAPTER SIX

UNDERSTANDING YOUR BELIEF SYSTEM

HOW IT WORKS AND HOW YOU CAN MAKE IT WORK!

I f you have not yet read and signed the preceding agreement to this chapter, please STOP reading and go back and read, agree, date, and sign it now. Please do not play fast and loose with something you truly do not yet understand. If you want to receive 100% of all the benefits of what I have to teach you, you must follow 100% of all the steps.

Now that you have complied with my request, let's start your understanding of the BELIEF system.

Within the past two decades more breakthroughs have been discovered and more personal, professional, and economic growth has been experienced by the discovery of one fact. That fact is: you have a system within you that is as real as your digestive system, your circulatory system, your respiratory system, and your elimination system. It is called your BELIEF system.

For thousands of years we have been told by every great way-shower that has ever walked this planet that life demonstrates as we BELIEVE. The heads of every philosophy and major form of education have hailed the existence of our BELIEFS. They have also acknowledged our need to recognize, embrace, and honor our positive BELIEFS while eliminating those BELIEFS that are destructive or do not create value in our lives. Until now, one major piece of the puzzle has been missing. That piece is, HOW?

Much like the definitions of marketing versus sales, I searched for a definition for what a BELIEF really is. Because I could not find one, I designed one. Here it is:

> *A BELIEF is a thought that is intensified by an energy called emotion. This emotion CAUSES the formation of a BELIEF, which is a sub-field of consciousness (a program), within your consciousness (your mind). This BELIEF drives, controls, or influences your thoughts, feelings, emotions, and actions without the focus of your willpower. This condition will remain or continue until changed or eliminated by an equal or greater energy.*

I have some good news and some not-so-good news for you. The good news is that at least 50% or more of all of your BELIEFS were not installed or created by you. Now, here is your not-so-good news. Regardless of who or what installed your BELIEFS, they are still your BELIEFS! It really does not matter what your BELIEFS are, what really matters is your answers to the following questions:

- Do your BELIEFS serve you?
- Do your BELIEFS allow you to serve others?
- Do your BELIEFS allow you to be served?

If you answered "Yes" to each of these three questions, then by definition they are positive BELIEFS, because their results are positive. If you answered "No" to each of these three questions, then by definition they are negative BELIEFS, because their results are negative. If you have two yes answers and one no answer or two no answers and one yes answer, you have what is called a Marginal BELIEF. The easiest way to work with it is to look at it as "majority rules." If you have two yes answers and one no answer, treat this as a positive BELIEF. If you have two no answers and one yes answer, treat this as a negative BELIEF. This is important to you because you need to make a BELIEF one way or the other for a clear and measurable result. Remember, the clearer you are within your BELIEF system, the clearer your life will be personally, professionally, and economically.

Very soon, by studying what I teach you and applying what you learn, you will be able to identify, replace, or strengthen your BELIEFS anytime you choose. You will also be able to identify, replace, or strengthen the BELIEFS of others too. Here is a model I use to measure positive versus negative BELIEFS. These questions must be answered yes or no:

- *Does this BELIEF or its associative actions hurt you, limit you, or limit your life in any way?*
- *Does this BELIEF or its associative actions hurt anyone else, limit anyone else, or limit anyone else's life in any way?*
- *Does this BELIEF or its associative actions create value in your life?*
- *Does this BELIEF or its associative actions create value in anyone else's life?*

Along with identifying positive versus negative BELIEFS, you will also find the above model is a powerful tool for decision making.

It is my experience from working with thousands of people over many years, that each of us has thousands of both positive and negative BELIEFS. I have also observed that the more abundant the number of your positive BELIEFS, the more positive the results that you are able to demonstrate.

Conversely, the more voluminous your negative BELIEFS, the less positive the results you are able to demonstrate. Regardless of what you say you want and regardless of your willpower to have it, do it, or be it, your BELIEFS control your results.

I will outline for you in the following pages techniques to identify and strengthen your positive BELIEFS. I will also show you how to identify and replace your negative BELIEFS. It will be very helpful for you to revisit this chapter several times and repeat the exercises to continue to develop and strengthen your positive BELIEFS while you continue to identify and replace your negative BELIEFS. If you invest the effort, you will see dramatic results in just a few days!

YOUR BELIEF INVENTORY

Both positive and negative BELIEFS are relatively easy to identify and replace or strengthen when you know how. This process will require effort and practice on your part. However, everyone I have worked with and personally trained to do this, who really wanted to make powerful and positive changes in their personal, professional, and economic lives, have all succeeded at learning and applying these techniques. The *golden key* that unlocks your success with this, or anything else you really want to become great at, is to study, learn, Practice, Drill, and Rehearse (PDR).

The first step in identifying your BELIEFS is to look at the EFFECTS in your life and career. Let's begin with your positive BELIEFS. I am starting with your positive BELIEFS first because the energy that will result from them is positive and empowering.

Please notice that as you identify and strengthen your positive BELIEFS, you will feel much more positive. Do not be impressed, just remember that the feelings that you are experiencing are the result of focusing on your positive BELIEF. When you identify and begin to replace your negative BELIEFS, the feelings that you will experience are the result of focusing on your negative BELIEF. Do not give me the credit or the blame for the way you feel. Just be willing to do the work!

Please do not associate your positive or negative feelings with me. I am just your coach. As you experience the feelings that come from your positive BELIEFS, remember these feelings. When you identify and replace your negative BELIEFS, please remember that both sides of your BELIEF system generate the associated feelings that you have identified as positive or negative. In truth, these programs are neither positive nor negative, they simply generate feelings that you have associated as pleasurable or painful. Remember that some people have your identical negative BELIEF and experience it as a positive result or feeling. You are unique!

I am sure that you have heard the old saying, "One person's weakness is another person's strength." Many people have a BELIEF that says, "I am not safe flying." If you need to fly a great deal, you may want to change that BELIEF. If you don't need to fly, you may receive positive feelings that you perceive as pleasure because you BELIEVE that this "program" keeps you on the ground and safe. The *golden key* that unlocks your understanding is your personal view of your BELIEFS and the results you observe. If you enjoy the feelings, and the results are positive, or at least neutral, leave them alone. If you don't like the feelings or the results, you will now have the **success system** to change them.

Keep working until you have replaced **all** of the energy, feelings, and emotions that surround your negative BELIEFS. This is very important because if you still feel negative energy, you have not replaced the BELIEFS!

The following exercise is the best centering technique I have ever developed to help you stay in control of your own thoughts, feelings, and the associated results. You may find it helpful to read this process into a tape recorder and play it back with your eyes closed. The more real you can make this process, the more beneficial your results will be. This is where **you** must be 100% willing and disciplined to use your creative imagination. Make this exercise real!

Remember, also, that you need to do this process first thing in the morning. If you do, you will see a marked improvement in your thoughts, feelings, and their associated EFFECTS in your day. Many of my students report that this is the one technique that has helped them to manage their lives personally, professionally, and economically more than anything else they have ever used. (If you want to learn more, see the Resources Section in the back of this book.)

Remember, the more detail that you can add to make this process real, the better. If you have access to a solid table, put a chair at the head or Chairperson's position. Please go sit at a solid table now. If you have no solid table available to you right now, you can use anything solid like a book on your lap. Just pretend it is a table as you follow this exercise.

Imagine that you are in a magnificent boardroom. Notice all of the details of the opulent wall coverings. See the paintings that hang on the walls. Experience the rich and expensive carpet. Notice the ceiling with its unique and lavish lighting. This is the boardroom of your own brain. In the center of this boardroom is a long, beautiful, and ornate boardroom table. See the high back, lavish, and lush leather chairs all around the table. Walk to the head of the table and pull back the Chairperson's chair and see if anyone is sitting in your chair.

You might see a character that looks like a scared child sucking their thumb. You might see an angry old man or woman. If you have a weight issue, you might see someone that is overweight eating food. These characters, if any, represent that part of you that comes up and blocks you from effectively running your own life. When you are centered, clear, and balanced, nobody is in your chair!

If you see someone that looks like you, it is your ego reflection. After all, it could not be the real you because the real you is looking into the chair!

Now, with all of the authority, power, and control that you can muster, order them out of your chair! Say, **"Get out of my chair, now!"**

See them vacate your chair. Now, turn the chair around and sit in your chair. Turn the chair back towards the boardroom table. Feel the soft, rich leather surround you as you sink into your chair. Feel the power of being back in command of your own brain and life. Feel the complete and total balance return to your entire being.

Regardless of where your life has gone without you at the helm, feel the joy, excitement, and enthusiasm return now that you are back in total control. Now that you are back, you know that all of the results in your life will be World-Class. You are the boss of your own brain and life!

Look at each of the characters sitting in the chairs around the table. Connect with each of them. Take your time. After all, it is your life, your boardroom, your timetable, your brain. Take your time!

As you survey each person, see his or her discomfort as you look at each of them. Through your personal power, let them feel the knowledge, power, and control that exists within you. You have looked at the books, you have studied the records, and you know the truth. They have **not** done a good job of running your life while you've been gone. Through your demeanor and mental energy let them know that you know the facts and the truth! You have come back to take control and you're letting them know it, just like any great chief executive officer would do.

Sit back in your chair. Allow your vision to bring all of the different board members sitting around the table collectively into focus and say these words, like a commanding general, **"I'm back!"** Just look at how the power in those two words captures their complete and total attention.

Now say, "I have been gone for a long while, but I am here to tell you that **I am back!** In case anyone has any doubts, concerns, or misgivings as to why you are on this board, let me set the record straight. You are here to cooperate with each other individually and with me collectively. Together we will build this life that has **my name** on it into a whole new

Dynamic Dimension of what is possible. **I am back** at the helm and I'm staying at the helm. If any of you cannot or will not give 100% of what it will take for me to see, hear, feel, and experience the fulfillment of what I know is possible for this life I own, please raise your hand so that I can fire you personally!"

Notice that no hands are raised. Then say, "Very good. Now, go to work knowing that I expect and will accept only 100% positive results from you, from this moment on. We are going to have this same meeting every day and you are hereby notified that when and if I notice any of you whining or not giving 100%, you will be replaced immediately!"

Now, slap the table in front of you and say these words out loud, **"And so it is, and so it will be from now on. This meeting is adjourned!"**

Powerful technique isn't it? If you were in one of my live workshops where I do this exercise, I would see the same look on your face I always see on everyone else's face that really allows themselves to participate fully. The look I am describing is a centered peace, confidence, and surety that comes from you being fully present and in control of your own life. I do not care who signs your paycheck, when it comes to your life, **you** are the boss! You are also 100% responsible for all of your results, positive and negative. Even though some of those BELIEFS sitting around that boardroom table you did not install, you are, however, still responsible for their results. The great news is that you can replace them and I will show you how!

Just like any company reorganization of which I have been a part, our first step to the desired results is to identify, strengthen, and work with the people, in this case BELIEFS, which can and will produce the positive results you need. Once you have accomplished an increase in positive results and performance, you will have an increase in working capital. Once the working capital increases, you now have both the time and the resources to go to work on your "weak links." Just like fixing what once was a strong, efficient, and powerful logging chain, after you identify the weak links, the next step is to cut them out and replace them with new, solid, and powerful links. This is the only way to pull your load faster, farther, and more efficiently!

For this next exercise you will need some writing paper. I suggest a journal or at least a spiral bound notebook. From this point forward, please date and put the time on each of your writings. As you do more and more of this work you will notice patterns that show up in your writing. You will see that there are times of the day that you are more open and receptive.

I strongly suggest getting up an hour earlier than normal to do your BELIEF Replacement Training work. Remember that all great chairpersons of every board do what is needed without listening to the "timekeeper" on their board. If your timekeeper just whined, "But I cannot get up an hour earlier because, blah, blah, blah," say, "Be quiet or I will fire you and get someone that will help me find the time I need. I am the Chairperson and I know what is and is not needed!"

Remember that in your brain's "boardroom," you are the boss! You, as the Chairperson of the Board of your own brain, need to get fed as much encouraging, warm, loving, and powerful "brain food" as possible. You will find my *Good Morning, Let's Make it a Great Day!* And *Good Night, Sleep Right* audiocassette tapes very helpful in building your inner strength. (If you want to learn more, see the Resources Section in the back of this book.) I designed these tapes to be hooked up to a timer and tape player. As you go to sleep, the *Good Night, Sleep Right* tape relaxes your body as it feeds your mind with the pure, powerful, and positive reinforcements you need to reach and stay in control. *The Good Morning, Let's Make It A Great Day* tape slowly helps you to wake up in the morning. It gently and gradually increases your brain waves so you increase your power to take command of another day as Chairperson of the Board! I first created these tapes to help me achieve these same benefits. You will be amazed and delighted how great they work!

You will not notice and enjoy the **automated** response from all of your brain board members until you do this work for at least 63 days (three rounds of 21 days). We all need help obtaining the right tools and learning how to use them. Remember that you must be willing to be new at this process and therefore not good at it, until you get fair at it. You must further be willing to be fair until you get good. You must tolerate being good at something, until you become excellent at it. If you don't stop at excellent you will surely reach World-Class!

There are as many **altitudes** or levels as there are **attitudes** of mind about them. I call the altitudes Dynamic Dimensions. These Dynamic Dimensions are: Fair, Good, Excellent, and World-Class. Attitudes are like suits of clothes we wear. Some are bright, attractive and useful. Others are dark, dingy, and tattered. Some attitudes are positive and

CAUSE the results we want and that we take credit for. Some attitudes are negative and CAUSE the results we don't want and that we blame something or someone else for. Remember that you choose your attitude, just like you chose the clothes that you are wearing right now. If you don't like the way your current attitude is causing you to feel, choose again!

To understand Dynamic Dimensions better, look back at the Dynamic Dimension you experienced prior to the one you are in now. Notice how what appeared difficult for you then is easy for you now. Can you remember when you first started the job that you are now excellent at? Remember how uncomfortable you were when you first started? Welcome to your **current** Dynamic Dimension! Is there a Dynamic Dimension above excellent? Yes, it is called World-Class! It is truly a phenomenal way to work and live.

The first step is for you to prove to yourself that this **success system** works for **you** too. Your personal observation, demonstration, and experience of your own positive results are the only way to achieve this. Remember that positive, empowering results count!

By my own observation, demonstration, and experience, each of the Dynamic Dimensions that you will move into and experience will produce the results of the previous Dynamic Dimension. In other words, when you are in the dimension called **Fair**, your results will be **poor**. When you move into the Dynamic Dimension called **Good**, your results will be **fair**. **Excellent** brings you **good** results, and **World-Class's** compensation level is **excellent**! Why is this? The reason is so simple it will amaze you. In the learning process of any new skill, you will only receive the benefits and compensation of your previous education and skill's level. It is like going to school. When you enter college, you would not expect to draw a college graduate's income, would you? You earn at, or just above, the income of a high school graduate. When you enter your master's program, you earn a college graduate's income. When you enter your doctorate work you get a master's compensation. You will not get the doctorate's rewards and compensation until you **finish** your degree. Simple, isn't it?

I want you to think about a quality, talent, or ability that you have that is positive. It can be a simple thing like, "I'm a good salesperson!" It might be, "I'm a great mom or dad," or, "I'm a good teacher or manager." I want you to pick one thing that you are good at and which you BELIEVE that you are good at. Select a quality, talent, or ability that you would like to see increase its power and associated effects and benefits. Select any BELIEF that has a positive result.

Look for your first "I am good at" BELIEF. Take your time because I know it may be tough finding something at which you BELIEVE you are really good.

Now that you've been willing to see one thing that you are really good at, turn to a new sheet of paper in your notebook or journal. Answer these questions and stay in your Chairperson's chair! Do not allow any board member's BELIEFS to take control or to interfere with your thinking.

To help you understand how to determine if you have identified the core BELIEF, here are the four tests I have discovered to help you identify a BELIEF. For it to qualify as a BELIEF you must have one or more of these effects to confirm you are not just experiencing an associated emotion, feeling, or intellectual concept about yourself.

If one or more of these qualities are present, you are at a BELIEF program.

<u>Test 1.</u> *When you speak the words or phrase that identifies your* BELIEF, *you feel an emotional energy.*

When you have found or touched a positive BELIEF, you will feel a positive energy. The intensity you feel is in direct relation to your willingness to feel it, and the size of the BELIEF. Unfortunately, the males of our species have been taught to BELIEVE that it is not normal or acceptable to feel, experience, and express our emotions. Females, on the other hand, generally have the opposite BELIEF. Our society also supports our females by not judging them for feeling, experiencing, and expressing their emotions. This allows females to experience this process more easily.

If you are a male and have a BELIEF that it is not acceptable for you to feel, experience, and express your emotions, you need to know that nothing could be further from the truth. However, if you BELIEVE it, then your perception is your reality. Females have a distinct advantage in doing this work because they do not BELIEVE that feeling, experiencing, and expressing their emotions is wrong or makes them less feminine. However, we males can and must give ourselves permission to feel, experience, and express our emotions because complete satisfaction, total happiness, and true World-Class living is based on our emotions as well as our intellect. This is not to say that we men need to become unmanly. For now, just be willing to feel, know, and trust that when you touch the BELIEF, you will feel something. If you feel nothing, test #1 has failed.

There are three other tests that are intellectual in design that should make you male readers feel more comfortable. The good news, gentlemen, is you do not have to rely on just your feelings to determine whether or not you have discovered a BELIEF.

We all feel, and yet, we men need to develop our ability to feel, experience, and express our emotions to completely experience and fully express our **real** self. Gentlemen, just know and trust that I will walk you through the maze of your emotions to a safe and powerful place where you can feel, experience, and express your emotions without looking or being looked at like a "girly man." I have hundreds of very successful manly men that have grown and benefited from this work without giving up any of their masculinity.

Gentlemen, if you want to truly relate to the other 50% of human beings that occupy this planet (women), you need to understand what motivates them.

The BELIEF that "only **real** men feel, experience, and express their emotions" is a healthy example of successfully relating to our female counterparts. If you doubt me, just ask any woman that appeals to you. She will, based on her feelings that you really want to know, tell you that what I just said is the absolute truth. "Only **real** men feel, experience, and express their emotions!"

Test 2. *The effects or results of your BELIEF repeat themselves.*

You will notice that, on a regular basis, your BELIEFS and their associated results, both positive and negative, will repeat themselves over and over again. Even in the examination of a positive BELIEF you will notice that the same test is valid.

Let's say one of your positive BELIEFS is, "I'm a great salesperson!" As you look back over your history, you will see that time and time again this BELIEF came out to serve you and perhaps save you. After closing a difficult sale, you either thought or expressed your BELIEF, "I'm a great salesperson!" In the times where you have been challenged as to your performance, this BELIEF has come to your defense, echoing through your mind and perhaps out of your mouth, "But, I'm a great salesperson!" Sometimes you may have even been called egotistical for your recantation of your BELIEF. It is **not** your ego; it is your BELIEF.

<u>Test 3.</u> *When the BELIEF is expressed, it seems unusual to the observer but makes perfect, logical sense to the BELIEVER.*

Once again let's say your BELIEF is, "I'm a great salesperson!" However, you are currently in a sales slump. If you share your BELIEF with your sales manager, he or she will look at you like a "pool full of carp!" They do not get it. This is why you need to keep this work to yourself until you have produced unquestionable results.

Once your positive BELIEF has been fortified, doubled, or even tripled in strength, your results will speak for themselves. I will then show you how to use these empowering results to build your positive BELIEF and your results even stronger! We both know that when you have focused all of your energy and attention on what you have wanted and needed in the past, you **always** got the results you wanted and needed, true? Now is the time to use those same disciplines again to automate your success!

<u>Test 4.</u> *You defend, explain, or justify your BELIEF.*

When questioned or challenged about your BELIEF, notice what you tend to defend. You may notice that you say things like, "Yes, but," or "Let me explain," or "You don't understand," when you are challenged about your BELIEF.

No one really cares what you BELIEVE. They do not understand and they do not want to understand. They simply want the results which are important to them. Stop defending yourself and realize that you are experiencing thoughts, feelings, emotions, and actions that are expressing themselves without the focus or control of your willpower. In other words, a BELIEF!

The time to start learning is now. If you do not, you will stay on the same "treadmill" you have been on most of your life. Stay in your Chairperson of the Board chair and decide to do this work to free yourself, your life, and your career from the same results that motivated you to get this book in the first place. If you do, you will be amazed and delighted with the results. You are the boss of your own brain; start acting like it and do the work to get the consistent, automatic results you need and deserve. It is absolutely a fact that you can automate success in every area of your life. As Chairperson of your own brain, you know this is the truth! You have done it before. Now we are going to make success automation permanent!

Like any coach worth being coached by, I need to know that you will take positive action in the direction that you say you want and need to go. I know you will thank me for "nudging" you in the right direction when you see, experience, and enjoy the benefits of doing this vital work.

Think of BELIEFS as "programs" in your mental computer. They were installed primarily to protect you from pain or harm. Much like a box of baby clothes that you have long outgrown, they are now choking you! You would not look at the baby clothes and say, "Bad clothes, bad clothes, bad clothes!" You have just outgrown the "clothes" BELIEFS and it is time to release and replace the Negitroid ones and build, develop and strengthen the Positronic ones.

I understand that you may not yet fully understand or grasp the importance of your BELIEFS or how to release, replace, or strengthen them. At this point, all you need to do is trust that if you already understood all about this subject, you would not be having any doubts or confusion. If you can grasp the understanding of that point, you can and will take a quantum leap forward by understanding the answer to this following question; what separates you from the people you admire who have the consistent results that you seek?

It is **not** product knowledge. You have close to or even more product knowledge than the top performers you admire, true? It is **not** personality. You have as good or even a better personality than the consistent high achievers you know, correct? It is **not** your size, race, or gender. Consistent high achievers come in all sizes, all ages, all races, and in each gender, valid? It is **not** formal education. Steve Jobs, the founder of Apple computer and successful by at least economic standards, did not finish college. Bill Gates, the founder of Microsoft and now the richest man in the world, dropped out of college, too!

Your BELIEFS are the difference. Large, strong, powerful, and positive BELIEFS are what separate the stars from the darkness! "Okay Steven, so where do I go from here and what do we do next?" Oh, how I love the sound of a freshly opened mind! The old saying is true, "Your mind is like a parachute, it only works when it is open!"

Open your notebook or journal to a new sheet of paper. At the top of the sheet of paper write a brief statement that describes your positive BELIEF. Under your BELIEF write this question. "If I BELIEVED this positive BELIEF twice as strongly as I BELIEVE it now, how will it impact every area of my life and what will my entire life look like?" Answer this question in as much detail as possible. *Please stop reading now and do this exercise!*

I hope you stopped reading and did the exercise. If not, please do it now. Nothing else I teach you will make any sense or bring you the results you want if you do not do this exercise. Please do each step as we go along and you will see the results that you want. This technique is very powerful at the subconscious level of your mind. You are "sowing a new crop" that will bear a wonderful and bountiful harvest. However, for any crop to grow, you must first get the seed into the ground.

Provide a separate page for each area of your life that you want to improve. Let's work on your career first. Write *Job Performance.* Now write these words under job performance: "If I BELIEVED this positive BELIEF twice as strongly as I BELIEVE it now, what would my job performance look like in just 30 days?" Write your answer in as much detail as possible.

Your second area is *Income.* Write these words under income. "If I BELIEVED this positive BELIEF twice as strongly as I BELIEVE it now, what would my income look like in just 30 days?"

Next, write *Health.* Then write this question, "How will I breathe, sit, walk, and talk if I BELIEVE this positive BELIEF twice as strongly as I BELIEVE it now? How will this BELIEF improve my health in just 30 days?"

Your next area is *Self-Esteem.* Write this question and the answer with as much detail as possible. "How would I feel about myself in just 30 days when I allow this positive BELIEF to expand to twice its current size and power?" Remember to answer the question in as much detail as possible.

Additionally, write *Self-Image.* Please write this question. "How will this increase in my self-esteem impact the way I think, talk, and feel about myself in just 30 days?" Again, add as much detail to your answer as possible.

The next area is *Relationships.* What I want you to do in this area is have one category for business relationships and one category for personal relationships. Give each set of these relationships a separate page. Please write this question: "What new and wonderful improvements will this new, super-sized, positive BELIEF do for my relationships in just 30 days?"

Please write, in as much detail as possible, what your new super-sized, positive BELIEF will do to enhance your business relationships in just 30 days. Then, in as much detail as possible, on a separate page, write what your new super-sized, positive BELIEF will do to enhance your personal relationships in just 30 days.

Repeat this same exercise **three times** over the next 24 hours. You will find it very helpful to provide a separate page for each area. Each time you return to each area over the next 24 hours you will see that your mind will identify new possibilities as your positive BELIEF actually expands. It is **critical** that you record each improvement as it shows up. It is equally important that you stay in your Chairperson's chair and do **not** allow any thoughts, feelings, or emotions to come from any of your "board members."

The last exercise for today, other than PDR, is for you to write the following Positronic Mind Affirmation (PMA) on a separate 3x5 card. It is important that you carry this card with you **everywhere** you go. If you truly want your positive BELIEF to expand and if you want to receive the benefits from it, please read this affirmation **out loud** three times a day. You need to read this PMA first thing after awakening in the morning, before you eat your noon meal, and just before you go to sleep at night. Here is where you need to apply your creative genius and your self-discipline. See, hear, and feel yourself already in possession of this magnificent increased positive BELIEF.

Hear yourself speak the words and allow the words to resonate within you. See yourself, as the **real** and newly empowered **you,** expressing and receiving everything you want at a faster, larger, and more abundant rate. This is where you must stay in your Chairperson's chair. Remember that **you** are the boss of your own brain. Any other voices, feelings, or votes contrary to this new and powerful truth about **you** must be stilled or quieted by **you.**

You would not allow anyone, even a friend or relative, to come in and judge or disrupt your home or family, would you? Then do not allow your old brain tapes to voice their judgement, criticism, or condemnation now either. This is a path that you have chosen and it is working. Stay with it!

If you will trust and follow my coaching for the next 21 days, you will have so much evidence to override any other voice within you that you and I will sing a success duet together for the next 21 days. By the end of 42 days, you will so clearly see, hear, and feel the abundant results that you will be able to sing a magnificent solo for the third 21 days. You will have all of the skills and abilities to sing solo for the rest of your life! It will not be long before you will be teaching others to sing their own success solo.

Please copy the following PMA to a separate **3x5 card**.

Here is your PMA

The POWER *I feel within me IS the real me, and IS who and what I really am! I feel my newly inspired, positive* BELIEF *growing and expanding. I hear it speaking through me now, stronger than ever before! I see new smiles reflected back to greet mine. I feel a wonderful new sense of joy, peace, and confidence that is mine. I command all other thoughts, feelings, emotions, and* BELIEFS *to "Be still!" I am in control of my own mind. I choose this new empowered path for my life. I receive, acknowledge, and accept all of the wonderful rewards and demonstrations of my expanded* BELIEF, *and I record them in my journal as the demonstrations of the new me that they truly are. I feel a new sense of pride that humbles me, as I know that I am now becoming who and what I've always wanted to be. I say, "Thank you" to myself and to all that have helped me on this new and magnificent path of understanding and accomplishment. And so I go, and so I grow, and so I am!*

Please carry this **3x5 card** and PMA with you everywhere you go. It will become one of your new brain board members. As this BELIEF grows, expands, and gains strength and power, you **will** see and experience the equivalent results. It is very important that you record each of these results in your notebook or journal regardless of how small or insignificant you think they are. Just do it! As this work progresses, you will see why this is important.

Mark your calendar for a minimum of 21 days forward. Remember, you cannot use this PMA too long, but you can use it for too short of a time! Again, it is vital that you do not share this information or process with anyone until you are at the end of your third 21-day cycle (63 days). If you do, you will learn the hard way that even well-meaning, but ignorant, family members and friends or business associates will express their opinions about what you are doing. You have probably experienced this in the past. Their opinions are almost always negative. Remember, if they are so smart, how come they are **not** successful in **all** areas of their lives?

In my experience, I have found basically only three types of people. I call them: *Positrons, Nutrobots* and *Negitroids.* As you grow and develop your skills, abilities, and talents through developing your BELIEF system, you will notice that you will get all kinds of friendly advice. Notice also that you will seldom, if ever, get negative input from Positrons.

You will never hear, "Be careful about losing too much weight," from people who are thinner than you are. You will never hear, "Don't work too hard," from people that are more successful than you are. Do not put yourself at risk of being pulled off your success track until you are strong enough and can put down the biggest Negitroid with overwhelming evidence that what you are doing works, BIG TIME!

I also caution you to not try to help other people yet. You are not yet strong enough to withstand the avalanche of "their stuff" that you **will** experience. The best and only way for you to help others now is to be a Positronic example of what is possible. If anyone asks you how you have made such incredible advances in your personal, professional, and economic lives in such a short time, just tell them that you are taking a new professional development course. Also tell them that you do **not** choose to discuss the details of the course until you have completed it on (whatever date equals 63 days from your starting date). If they press you for more information, and many will, simply look at them and ask this question, "What part of 63 days from now was I not clear about?" End the conversation right there! Many people want to arrive without making the trip! Remember this Steven Lloydism.

> ## "The man or woman at the top of the mountain did not fall there!"

Resolve from this day forward to require **everyone** in your life to do the work that is required to get the results that you are working so hard to achieve. I cannot help coach you to become a World-Class achiever if you are going to continue to require yourself to carry other people on your back. This race called life is hard enough to win running solo. This does not mean that if you, like me, get real excitement and satisfaction from helping others, that you cannot or should not help others. Just trust and know that you really cannot help others until you have their full attention, interest, and commitment to do the work to become a real World-Class achiever. That is not possible for you yet until we get each area of **your** life working so well and so successfully that your natural excitement and enthusiasm CAUSES you to start "wearing-out your clothes from the inside" with natural excitement! Everyone's attitude is contagious, the question you need to ask yourself of everyone you meet is, "Is his or her attitude worth catching?"

This is an exciting day for you, enjoy and **celebrate** it! You have already worked hard. Your brain needs to feel the passion of the victory dance. When you celebrate your victories, regardless of how small, your brain wants more and more of this new and powerful **success system**. So, for today, stop reading and give your brain a chance to absorb what you have already read. I will see you tomorrow!

DAY TWO OF YOUR NEW SUPER-SIZED BELIEF

So, how did you do with your exercises for day one? Did you carry your 3x5 card with you everywhere you went? Did you read your PMA at least three times during the day?

Please answer these questions knowing that you cannot escape the truth. Did you give 100% effort to each of the steps as I outlined them? Did you get a noticeable result that you recorded in your notebook or journal? Did you have at least three or more experiences of the benefits from your positive BELIEF that you associated with your new expanded BELIEF? Do you see the relationship between effective effort and your results?

Your brain and your BELIEFS are very much like any other muscle group in your body. If you and I went into a gym and I coached you on developing one specific muscle group, you **would** notice a result the very next day.

As a World-Class coach, my objective is for you to see and feel the results without experiencing pain to the point that you do not show up for day number two! Here is yet another Steven Lloyd-ism.

> *"Your pain is in direct proportion and relationship to your resistance to the lessons you need to learn!"*

There's no quick fix or effortless process to get where you say you want and need to be. Here's some more great news. Your brain, much like the muscles of your body, will very soon start to enjoy this process and request more and more of the same. Just as if I was coaching you in exercise, you get to decide how far you want to take the mental success coaching process.

Like fitness, perhaps you will be happy with a level of mental BELIEF development that will allow you to simply enjoy your life more. Some people have a physical fitness goal that is satisfied when they are in good enough shape to not have to stop to catch their breath when they walk up a small flight of stairs. If that is your goal, that is fine with me. Just do not allow one of your negative brain board members to speak through your lips and say something like, "Yes, I read Steven Lloyd's books and I did not get any of the great results he talks about!"

I told you from the beginning, my work is not designed to increase your reading, listening, watching, or workshop attending skills. You are already a World-Class observer. Other than an educational tax deduction, you may not have gained very much from the other courses you have studied. Let me be very clear here. My job is coaching you, and your job is doing the work to get you where you say you want to be. If you get done before I do, please raise your hand! I did not create the basic law of the universe, CAUSE and EFFECT. I am just reporting it to you as it relates to your personal, professional, and economic growth and development. So, let's go back to the gym and start your second workout.

Regardless of what kind of results you have received from day one, you can and must do more to get more. At some level within you, your Chairperson knows and understands what you can and must get from this education. You really can automate the skills, strategies, techniques, and systems of your personal, professional, and economic lives to demonstrate World-Class success.

Following is a chart that shows what your BELIEF looked like before we started this **expansion** process. In just 21 days, your new **super-sized** BELIEF can equal or even exceed the result you want.

The fact is that you cannot consistently and automatically achieve your desired results until your BELIEFS are equal to or greater than the results you want.

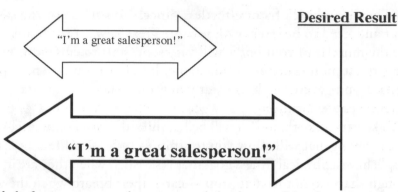

Your belief must measure the extent and the degree of the desired result. Big belief, big result!

Think back to when you were first learning to drive a car. Just for a moment, become that 16-year-old kid again. Imagine you're behind the steering wheel of the car in which you learned how to drive. Recall all of your feelings of excitement and fear that increased your sense of awareness, ego, and transition into adulthood. Really let yourself be that 16-year-old kid again.

Now, recall how all of your attention was placed on the hundreds of details needed to successfully navigate yourself from point A to point B and beyond. Recall your feelings, emotions, and your BELIEFS as you remember yourself as this 16-year-old student driver approaching your first controlled intersection and you are at the wheel. Remember thinking, "I know the light is going to change from green to red!" Remember how the light stayed green and stayed green and stayed green and then, sure enough, almost as if your thoughts were controlling the signal light, the light turned to yellow and then red.

Do you recall all of the thoughts pouring through your head all at the same time? Thoughts like, "I need to ease off the gas so I don't jerk the car. Now, push on the brake, no, no that's not hard enough, I'm not going to stop in time, push harder!" Can you experience the feeling of taking that successful breath when everything turned out okay? Remember feeling yourself settling back into the seat feeling really proud of yourself only to hear the horn of the car behind you honking to remind you that the light has changed back to green?

Okay, you can come back from your nightmare of learning how to drive. Think now in the same detail about your current driving skills, abilities, talents, BELIEFS, and results. Do you even think about it anymore?

Do you find yourself thinking, "Okay, now the key goes into the ignition this way?" Or, "Push the gas pedal once to activate some gas into the ignition chamber, put your foot on the brake, okay, turn the key, oh great it started!" Of course not! You do not even think about any of these steps and probably have not thought about them for many years. You are just like everyone else who automatically goes from point A to point B on automatic pilot. Heck, by now, you can probably do morning tasks like shaving or putting on eye makeup while you drive and talk on your cell phone all at the same time!

Wouldn't you like to put every single important area of your life and career on this kind of **success automatic pilot**? Well, that is exactly what we can and will do. Remember, automatic pilot alone is not the desired result. **Success automatic pilot** is the result you want and need.

In many areas of your life you are already on automatic pilot. Notice that I did not say **success automatic pilot**. Remember a few years back when an airliner crashed into a mountain, killing everyone on board. The pilot never took the airplane off automatic pilot! It has happened more than once and it happens with people too. You must do course inspections and corrections as you move forward on your personal, professional, and economic journeys.

I fly a great deal and I feel very safe, however, every chance I get, I say to the captain, "Remember to turn off the automatic pilot when you are supposed to!" They always laugh, but they also lose their grin when they see that I am serious.

Your BELIEF system is **your** automatic pilot. The walls that you keep bumping into are your negative BELIEFS telling you to ignore the warning signals and keep flying. Please continue to listen to, feel, and look at all of your BELIEFS and replace the ones that no longer serve you.

The challenge I observe when I do private coaching for individuals who claim they are "sick and tired of feeling sick and tired," is that they are usually stuck in their story. If you hear from other people that they have "heard your story," you have allowed your ego to occupy your Chairperson's chair. The ego is that whiner/controller that does not want you to succeed. It will never accept responsibility for anything that goes wrong in your life. It does, however, claim all of the credit for what your Chairperson achieves!

You can recognize the ego's voice because it says words like, "Their fault," when it looks at the problem or for someone to blame. I know you have either worked with or for someone whose ego caused a problem but would not accept the responsibility. I saw a great cartoon that showed a pompous type character standing at the front of a room of people saying, "And I would like to say that I have had a wonderful year claiming credit for all of the ideas of all the people who work for me." Egomania is an unusual disease; it makes everyone sick except the one who has it! Your ego is too busy taking and seeking credit to give any away.

There are also feelings, smells, and tastes that you can recognize as the differences between these two internal characters (ego and Chairperson) that are always fighting for the control seat within you. The feelings that come out of your ego, following achievement, feel very similar to an artificial high, like drinking too much caffeine. Your Heart or Chairperson's chair gives feelings of being centered, peace, teamwork, and a knowing that you have done and or said the right things for the right reasons.

Recall the words your Chairperson uses. Your Chairperson refers to you, as, "**You** or we." Your Chairperson says things like, "**You** did really good there," or, "It is important that we really pay more attention to this or that because **we** are not getting the results **we** want." Your Chairperson is the one who gives other people praise. You will also notice that your Chairperson uses exterior focused words like, "You really did a good job on that, Jack," or, "You know, Sally, you are really fun to work with!"

Your job is to continue to remain in control of the board of your brain by doing the Chairperson technique exercise every single morning for 63 days. It will continue to put you in, and keep you in, the Chairperson's chair. Therefore you will stay in control of your own thinking. Do this exercise two or even three times a day if necessary. Do this exercise as often as needed until you are comfortable and familiar with being back in charge of your own brain and all of the associated results.

Remember that the first 21 days only starts to build and expand your new Super-Sized BELIEF. The second round of 21 days reinforces and expands your BELIEF and your results even more. The third round of 21 days develops your abilities to **automate** each area of your life into **success automatic pilot**. Keep in mind that like any good pilot you must keep inspecting and correcting to attain the results that you want. All of your BELIEFS need to be inspected every 21 days to make sure the results that you are getting are still what you want. If not, you need to replace the ones that are the CAUSE of the EFFECT you do not want. This book will give you all of the tools you need to replace negative BELIEFS with positive BELIEFS that will bring you the life and career that you want. Remember that you cannot get to 30,000 feet if you only use enough brain fuel to stay on the ground at the airport! Also, know that 30,000 feet is only your cruising goal. Currently you might think you would always enjoy flying high with the good life. This is where you need to trust me. You will get very bored sitting back with your arms folded in your high back leather Lazy Boy Chairperson's chair if you do not challenge yourself.

You NEED to understand all of the altitudes (levels) on the journey to your destination. You NEED to thoroughly know your capacity. Just for fun, every now and then (say, every 21 days), you NEED to take yourself through some new maneuvers just to see what your new high-powered BELIEFS are capable of. This will happen as soon as you understand the answer to one of the most powerful questions you will ever be asked: why do you NEED to accomplish what it is you say you want? I trust you are sincere in your desire for personal, professional, and financial growth, development, and advancement. If you are, I am about to take you on one of the most beneficial journeys you will ever take. When you master the next chapter, you will see how really simple it is to get whatever you want. In the next chapter you will discover that you can have everything that you have ever wanted. All you have to do is be willing to NEED it!

CHAPTER SEVEN
The Power of Need

N ow that you have identified a positive BELIEF and you are doing
your daily exercises to build it into a *super-size* BELIEF, it is time
to show you what you can really do!

Until now you have had no idea that you were sitting on enough
rocket fuel to launch your life and career into orbit! This is a great day.
From this day forward you will never look at your capabilities the same
way again. Following today you will never try to find your name on a
sales production chart again. You will be **setting the pace** for others to
follow instead of trying to just keep up. So here is another small and simple, but required, exercise for you. Take out your appointment calendar
and circle today and write these words in the circle, "The day I found the
secret to my current success!"

Over the past 18 years I have had the privilege of interviewing many
of the top World-Class people in several walks of life, business, and
industry. Without exception I have noticed that each one KNEW the
answer to WHY they were operating at such a high level. They also had
transcended the dimension of want into the Dynamic Dimension of
NEED.

Ask yourself this question. If you had all of the money that you think that you could ever want, how long would it take for you to start getting bored? Before you answer, "I would never get bored," think long and hard about the question I just asked you. Let me repeat the core of it again. How long would it take for you to **start** getting bored?

Regardless of how wonderful you may think a lifestyle is that you have never experienced, just think about the things you enjoy and take for granted that someone else would see as abundance. You do not have to look too far below your current circumstances to find someone who thinks you live like royalty! Do you realize that if you live in a building that keeps you dry and warm, have a television that works and a car that takes you from point A to point B, that you already live better than 90% of the people in the world?

Most people who struggle with not having enough money BELIEVE that tons of money will solve all of their problems and make them happy. There are thousands of case histories to prove that just the opposite is true. Lots of money brings lots of responsibilities and revelations. It is akin to wanting some of your favorite ice cream so badly you can hardly stand it. Then, one day, you can afford to eat it everyday. After a week or so, you get a little tired of it. The same is true with having lots of money. It does not feel at all the way you think it will when you finally get it.

Think back to your first car. Remember how badly you wanted that car? Until now I've not told anyone this story but when I got my first new car I slept in it the first night I brought it home! I do not think my feelings, emotions, and actions were that much different from anyone else who just got a brand new car. Remember how often you washed that car the first three weeks or 21 days? Remember how careful you were with it, and how you worried about it for the first month?

Even though, like me, you may have had a long-term love affair with your first car too, think back, do you recognize the 21-day cycle pattern? I even named my car, but after 63 days (three 21-day cycles), I was no longer first in line at the car wash! After three months I was no longer walking all the way across the parking lot because I parked my car so far away from everyone else! This is normal. Everyone goes through the same experience. But ask yourself **why**? The answer is so simple that it will amaze you. Your level of desire and your level of familiarity dropped from NEED to **want**.

If you follow this downward human engineering cycle all the way to when you sold or traded that car, you will also see that your inner motivation went from **need** to **want**. From **want** to **like** and from **like** to **okay**. The last stage of the letting go process is from **okay** to **release**.

If you kept the car I am using in this example too long, you might have even experienced **okay** to **dislike**. Do you now see that we do this with every single relationship in both our personal and professional lives? After we attracted something or someone into our lives, if we are not careful, the human engineering cycle goes in the opposite direction too. When we want to release something or someone, the attraction cycle is simply reversed. The *golden key* to unlock the door of longterm successful experiences is to recognize these cycles within us and to take action to complete them before they erode into negative BELIEFS and memories.

Especially where personal and professional relationships are concerned, we need to constantly be aware of and attend to our relationships to be sure we are always giving what is NEEDED to keep them fresh and new. The reversal of the attraction cycle is caused by lack of awareness or neglect, more than any other reason.

If an experience or relationship is approaching the end, bring it to conclusion before you experience or CAUSE major pain. All you need to create a lasting negative memory is to have your once new car leave you stranded by the side of the road at midnight in the middle of nowhere. If you experienced enough pain, you might even develop a negative BELIEF about the brand of that car and never buy another one again! Lack of awareness or neglect of your options CAUSES many negative BELIEFS. Your lack of awareness or neglect is CAUSED by in-box thinking. In the car example above, your negative BELIEF may have been CAUSED by your neglecting your car's maintenance. In other words, it may not have been the car at all. It may have been your lack of awareness or neglect of the maintenance requirements that are NEEDED for ongoing car success. There is always a way to succeed and you always have more options than you think you do. There are always at least three options, solutions, or correct answers to pick from on almost every issue, challenge, or question. You must first get out of your box long enough to see the other answers. Let me give an example of in-box and out-of-box thinking. Please answer the following question. What is half of 8?

I can just see you now. You are sitting there saying, "What a stupid question! There is only one answer and it is four!" You have successfully proven my point. You have just demonstrated in-box thinking. You will also never find the other two correct answers, if you stay in that box. Allow me to help you out of your box.

Look again at both the question and the possible correct answers. Draw an 8 on a piece of paper in your notebook or journal. Is or is there not a top and a bottom half of the eight? The only correct answer is yes. Cover up the top half of the eight and you will discover that your second correct answer is zero! Is there or is there not a left and a right half of the eight? Cover up the left half of the eight and you will discover that your third correct answer is three. Isn't out-of-box thinking fun? Please promise me that you will stay out of your box and in your Chairperson's chair from now on!

I took you on this little out-of-box thinking side trip for a very important reason. For you to experience and demonstrate World-Class results, you must look at your life and career from outside the box!

Let me ask you an easy question which has a simple yes or no answer and no out-of-box thinking required. Do you have everything in your life that you really BELIEVE you NEED? If you answered "No", you do not really BELIEVE you NEED it. I am not talking about something you may want, I am referring to what you NEED. Do you have a place to live that meets your NEEDS? How about food and clothing NEEDS? Do you have transportation NEEDS covered? How would you like to convert your wants into demonstrations that come to you with the same certainty as obtaining what you currently NEED? Well, keep reading and you too will discover the secret!

There is an old story about a young man who seeks the wisdom of an old wise man. The young man asked the wise man, "What is the secret of success and how do I attain it?" The old sage calmly looked at the young man and said, "Do you know how to find the river of Truth?" The young man said, "Yes, it runs along the bank near my village." The old wise man asked, "Do you know where the river forks into the river of Opportunity and the river of Responsibility?" The young man assured the teacher that he knew of the spot described. The old man said, "Meet me at the spot where those two rivers fork at sunrise tomorrow and I will give you the knowledge that you seek."

The young man thanked the old teacher and left feeling excited. The next morning the young man arose extra early and made his way in the darkness to be at the fork of the two rivers at sunrise. It was a moonless morning and the young man could not see more than a few feet ahead. When he reached the spot on the shore where the river of Truth forked and became the river of Opportunity and the river of Responsibility, the old wise man was not yet there. The young man sat down on the river-bank and waited.

As the sun pierced the predawn darkness the boy looked up and down the riverbank for the old way-shower. The wise man was still not there. The young man mentally returned to his meeting the day before to rethink carefully about the teacher's instructions. The sun was now just breaking the eastern sky. It was officially sunrise. Just as the young man had the thought of the exact instructions given to him by the old sage the day before, the young man's eyes moved to the exact spot where the river of Truth forked into the two rivers. There was the old man wait-ing patiently for the young man to come out of his self-imposed trance and come to the **exact** spot that he was instructed.

The young man jumped off the riverbank and moved through the waist deep water as fast as he could until he reached his teacher. The wise man smiled warmly, not speaking of the boy's lack of compliance. He looked at the young man and said, "Ask your request again." The young man spoke very clearly, "What is the secret of success and how do I attain it?" The wise man extended his arms just under the water, his face shining brightly as he said, "Lie back in my arms and I will give you the wisdom you seek." With his arms extended just under the water, he motioned for the young man to lie back in his arms. The young man moved toward his teacher with no fear. He laid back in his teacher's arms. The old man said, "Do you completely and totally trust me?" The young man said, "Yes, I do!" The old sage said, "Then take a deep breath." The young man did as he was instructed and as soon as his lungs were filled with air and his mouth was closed the old man pushed the young man deeply under the water.

The young student laid under the water for a minute or so not resist-ing. Soon, as the oxygen in his lungs was used up he started to struggle with his teacher to come to the surface. The old sage held him steadfast under the water. The young man fought with the old man to get to the fresh air. The old master was more than just wise, he was very strong. The young man thrashed and floundered to get to the surface. The old man pushed him deeper yet. The young man pushed himself from the river bottom up through the old teacher's greatest effort to restrain him. The young man gasped for breath and heaved for yet more air.

Finally, the young man's breathing returned to normal. He looked at the wise old man and said, "When I want success as much as I NEEDED to breathe, I will have it, right?" The old man grinned and said, "You not only have your answer, you also have wisdom as well!"

Your mind is the most powerful success-generating plant in the world. Everything you see, hear, or can touch was created or enhanced by a brain just like yours. The Coastal Redwoods in California and the Grand Canyon in Arizona are examples of naturally created wonders where human minds enhanced the ability for you and I to see and experience them. You would have never seen pictures of the great wonders of the world if some other brain had not NEEDED to develop the thing we use to enjoy them. If you look at everything that is unique, including the very book you are reading now, you will, if you look deep enough, find the NEED that created it. Take everything you currently value and follow it all the way back to the CAUSE and you will find that the EFFECT was driven by a NEED for it to happen or for it to be created!

There are two types of NEEDS: Those that create and those that destroy. You do not have to look very far or very deep to see examples of both. Look within yourself and within your own life and you will see both. Now, do not look too long or too deep. I want you to keep your focus on the positive and the creative. Just look at all of the NEEDS you have in your life that have created or attracted what you have. Others that do not have them would call them wants or luxuries but you see them as NEEDS and BELIEVE that you cannot, or will not, do without them. Are you starting to see the NEED for them?

It was not long ago that cell phones and pagers were only considered a NEED for professionals. Now, in cities all across America, the telephone companies have had to add hundreds of new area codes just to accommodate the expanded NEED for the millions of new cell phones and pagers that are now NEEDED by almost everyone.

I remember when I saw someone wearing a pager and knew that they were a doctor or someone really important who dealt with life and death issues. Today, businessmen look like a *Star Wars Jedi Knight* wearing a weapons belt! It is common to see a man wearing two pagers and a cell phone on his belt. I have seen ladies purses and briefcases with cell phones and pagers clipped on the outside like magnetic message notes hanging on a refrigerator!

I now open all of my workshops with a reminder to put all cell phones and pagers on silent mode or to turn them off. I am a member of the National Speaker's Association (NSA) where I have heard most of my professional speaker colleagues echo the same concerns. Even with the "Please do no interrupt this meeting with your NEED to communicate" reminder, it is common for someone not to follow those instructions. Not only do they interrupt the workshop with their lack of compliance, I have actually had people answer their cell phones and converse during the workshop!

What CAUSES people to do that? The answer is simple, as are most answers to most human engineering questions. These people BELIEVE that their NEED to communicate with someone else is greater than their NEED to participate in the workshop. They also have other human NEEDS, like the NEED for attention.

I have a technique that seems to work to get people to cooperate without making them angry. No World-Class teacher who has a goal of helping you learn really wants to make you angry.

Keeping in mind all of the possible NEEDS of the entire audience, either I or the person who introduces me starts the meeting with the question, "Are there any medical doctors or health care professionals here that may get a life and death emergency cell phone call or page?" In a general session we often get a few hands. We then ask those people to trade seats with the person on the outside aisle so that they can leave the meeting if NEEDED. We then explain that what I'm about to teach is both deep and critical information. We explain that I will be teaching about human NEEDS. Everyone else is asked to turn his or her cell phones and pagers off or to silent mode. We explain to the audience that there may be someone in the audience that has a NEED for attention or a NEED to feel important. We further explain that one of the ways that these types of people get attention is to interrupt large meetings like this one by receiving audible pages or cell phone calls. We explain that if you are that type of person, just know that I will stop the workshop and whatever it is I'm teaching and ask everyone in the room to give you a standing ovation. This technique works almost 100% of the time. The one or two times that it has not worked, we have all had a lot of fun giving this person a standing ovation!

DISCOVERING YOUR WANTS

Now it is time for your next lesson. Write in your book, if this is your book, or in your notebook or journal if it is not, each thing that you would like to **have**, **do**, or **be**. You will notice the following three pages have been created for you to record each of your wants. There is a page for each area of your life. There is one page for all of the things that you would like to **have**. There is one page for all of the things that you would like to **do**. The third page is for all the things that you would like to **be** or **become**. For this exercise pretend I am the Wizard of Success and I have the power to grant you all of your wishes. I will grant you every wish, only if you are willing to take it to the level of human consciousness called NEED.

Remember that you get to the Emerald City one step at a time on the Yellow Brick Road. By the way, do you know why they called the Emerald City, the Emerald City? Because that is the color of the reflection of the sun shining off all of the money of the people who live there!

So, what is your first step? Write down all of your wants. Like with all of my exercises, **please STOP reading and do the exercise**. I cannot help you get what you want if you do not or will not define what those wants are. Here's another Steven Lloyd-ism for you.

"*You cannot achieve what you will not define!*"

I have developed some prompts for you. All you have to do is answer all of the questions. Keep digging until you have all of the questions answered on each of the following three pages. You will notice I have left the last line of each page blank with only the statement "I want" as a prompt. Also, notice the last line of each want starts with the word "Why." Do NOT answer this question during your want-finding exercise. I will come back to the why later in this chapter. Also, leave the box to the left of each want question blank until later. Later, I will instruct you when to fill these in.

Remember that you promised to stay in your Chairperson's chair from now on and to not allow any other thoughts to control your thinking. All you have to do is answer the questions and that is easy for any good Chairperson!

Things I Want to Have

☐ I want a savings account with $ _____ as a balance.

Why _____

☐ I want to earn $ _____ per month.

Why _____

☐ I want _____for my relationship.

Why _____

☐ I want _____for the important people in my life.

Why _____

☐ I want _____for my health.

Why _____

☐ I want _____as a home.

Why _____

☐ I want _____as a reputation.

Why _____

☐ I want to have _____

Why _____

Things I Want to Do

☐ I want to go to _____

Why _____

☐ I want to experience _____

Why _____

☐ I want to play _____

Why _____

☐ I want to hear _____

Why _____

☐ I want to taste _____

Why _____

☐ I want to feel_____

Why _____

☐ I want to see_____

Why _____

☐ I want to (do) _____.

Why _____

Things I Want to Be or Become

☐ In my personal life I want to be or become _____

_____

Why _____

☐ In my professional life I want to be or become _____

_____

Why _____

☐ I want my weight and body to be _____

_____

Why _____

☐ I want my monthly sales to be _____

Why _____

☐ I want my total debt to be _____

Why _____

☐ I want to become the following kind of person _____

_____

Why _____

☐ I want to become _____

_____

Why _____

How did you do with the three "I Want" exercises? As your coach, my job is to get you to do the work that brings you the World-Class results that you say you want and NEED. Please remember that 100% World-Class results cannot come from any effort less than 100%! I told you from the beginning that this was going to be a different kind of book. I fully believe that this book is one of the most time intensive, practical, and success-oriented textbooks you have ever read.

One of the advantages of being in one of my live workshops is that I get to measure or time each lesson to the point of your understanding, application, and compliance with each of the success principles, ideas, concepts, strategies, and **success systems** that I teach. The more hands on training you receive the better you will do with any training. This is why I offer my Training Courses as 12-month ongoing training and development programs to organizations. A sales manager facilitates each lesson to make sure that each student masters each one of the steps. This assists them to ascend gradually and sequentially to a World-Class level of performance. Books are good tools, but they require a great deal of **self-discipline** to follow each of the steps completely. (If you want to learn more, see the Resources Section in the back of this book.)

Most people do not know that Michael Jordan hired his own personal training coach. Like you, he knew he was excellent. Hopefully, **you** also want to be World-Class! None of us can ever be perfect. We can, however, all be excellent! If you are already excellent, or as you enter the Dynamic Dimension called excellence, you will soon notice that there are different and unique levels of excellence. As you move into the third level of excellence you will become aware of a Dynamic Dimension above excellence and that level is called World-Class. There are also at least three levels of World-Class.

I know for a fact that each person who entered and transcended the levels of each of the Dynamic Dimensions I have described, all did so by mastering the fundamentals of each dimension. I know this as a fact because I have made a lifelong study of these people and all of them taught mastering the fundamentals!

When you walk into a dark room, you know that you must flip the switch to add light to the darkness. However, you will only get the desired light you need by flipping the switch **every** time you walk into a dark room. I suggest to you that, at least in your own home, you have **automated** the switch-flipping process. It has now been integrated to the point of **success automatic pilot** in your mind. Just like driving your car, right? My objective is to help you get to that same level in every critical area of your life. The easiest and fastest way to reach success that I have discovered in the past 29 years of research and testing is to first help you discover what you want and then help you move your want to the level of NEED. Beyond the NEED comes the demonstration. You will soon see, in doing all of the exercises, that having everything you want is really simple. Please note that I did not use the word easy. Easy is a relative term that normally indicates little or no effort. Be willing to put in the effort and you will soon see how simple having what you want really is!

TURNING WANTS INTO NEEDS

The next exercise is critical to your personal, professional, and economic success. For this exercise to produce the kind of results you are looking for, it will take at least 30 minutes of uninterrupted time. If you do not have a full 30 minutes of time with no chance of being interrupted please save this lesson until you do.

Turn back to the three pages of your wants. Now I want you to answer the why questions for each of the three areas of **have, do,** and **be** or **become.** There is only one rule. You cannot write, "Because I want it" or any other non-emotional answer. Remember that this is your list and your life. Please sit squarely in your Chairperson's chair and answer each and every why question. **Please stop reading now and do this exercise.**

Once you have completed answering all of the why questions, go back to each of the pages and put a priority number in each of the boxes to the left of your wants. Please number them 1 to 10 with 1 being the most important. Again, **please stop reading now and do this exercise.**

You should now have all of the why questions answered. You should also have each of them numbered 1 to 10 with 1 being your most desirable want. Take out three, 3x5 cards. Find your number 1 want from each category. I want you to rewrite the want into a NEED on a 3x5 card, in the following new way:

I NEED _____ (Fill in your number 1 want.)

Now think of your new NEED and get a clear *picture* in your mind of exactly what your new NEED is. Activate your auditory cortex by *speaking* your NEED out loud. Activate your emotional cortex and really *feel* the NEED at the core of who and what you are.

Now, write these words on each of your 3x5 cards. "I NEED (fill in your new need) as badly as I NEED to breathe! Right now, this is the most important NEED in my life!"

There is only one rule to make this process successful. You can only have this NEED when you pay cash! If your NEED is a house or some other piece of expensive property, you are allowed to borrow up to but not longer than, 15 years. Your brain will find a way to bring you EVERYTHING it BELIEVES you NEED. If you doubt this, just look at your life. You have many things that 90% of the other brains on our planet think are luxury items. However, your brain says, "Heck no, I NEED them." If you do not add the "pay cash" NEED, you may get everything you want very fast; however, you will also demonstrate a tremendous amount of debt too. Develop the NEED to be debt free. It is a wonderful way to live!

You may not think of yourself as well-off, but again just answer these simple questions: Do you have a roof over your head that does not leak? Do you have a car that carries you from point A to point B? Do you have a TV that works? Then you have already demonstrated what 90% of the people in the world think of as luxury items!

You already have most, if not all, of the things that people that you call "rich" have. They just NEED bigger homes, nicer cars, a better education for their kids, and in some cases, but very few, better relationships!

I know you may have a negative BELIEF that says, "Money cannot buy happiness." Well, money buys tons more happiness than poverty ever bought! Money buys lots more freedom and peace of mind than little or no money will ever bring you. The person who came up with that Negitroid quote was suffering from a BELIEF that he or she would never have much money, therefore they created a negative BELIEF that became popular. As I said earlier, money will not satisfy you, but it will add to your happiness! What will CAUSE you a lot of unhappiness is debt!

Let me give you a perfect example of how well this NEED system is now working in my own personal, professional, and economic lives. In 1992, my wife and I divorced after 18 years of marriage.

For 18 years I had become accustomed to owning elaborate homes and giving my family the very best. When my son Jim was just a little guy, I joked about getting a certificate from Tonka toys saying that we were the first and only family in America to own every single toy they had ever made. Following my divorce I was not only broke, I was $56,000.00 in negative debt!

I recall walking my two kids through a park one morning and pointing out a man pushing a shopping cart full of aluminum cans. He was going through a trashcan looking for more cans. I said to my children, "That man is worth $56,000.00 more than your Dad." Jessica said, "That can't be true daddy, that man is pushing a shopping cart and you drive a really nice sports car!" I said, "Yes, but he is at $0.00 and I am $56,000.00 in the red as far as my net worth is concerned." This was a time of great change and I was very uncomfortable and very angry.

After navigating through the most negative emotional time of my life, I decided that what I had BELIEVED about money was wrong. I am a person who truly appreciates and respects the scientific approach to life. If a system works for someone else, I will try it. I knew that no one in his or her right mind would keep performing failed experiments over and over again and expect to succeed where they had already failed time and time again. I decided then and there to try new experiments. I discovered and successfully used this **success system**. Please BELIEVE that if I can do this, you can, too!

Within two years I was living in a four-level estate type home with multi-level outside decks, a sunken hot tub, an in-ground pool, on almost an acre of land with magnificent trees. I kid people that I would love to go on vacation if I could find a nicer place to go! However, I was still carrying significant debts. The difference was, my net worth was on the positive side.

I had started, built, and managed four companies at this point in my life. I decided to build another company using my new **success systems**. It worked better than I had ever dreamed possible. My company grew into the largest company of its kind in the world! And within another two years, I met the woman of my dreams and we married and are very happy. One of the many reasons I married Sherri was that she not only agreed with my new **success systems**, she fully embraced them. She was as eager to benefit and grow from it as I was. Every day has been like a new and exciting adventure for us.

On May 11, 1996, our wedding day, we collectively developed a NEED to be completely debt free within 60 months. Considering the estate type home I described earlier, as well as the other things we both had accumulated, we had a lot of debt. At the time we were married, I was only able to take just enough money out of my company to barely get by. Nonetheless, this became a **white heat** passion for both of us. Sherri worked full-time and so did I. None of the typical avenues of money appeared to be the solution to our NEED.

I had already applied this new **success system** with excellent results, so I knew that it would work. We decided to sit down and intensify our NEED and spoke of it as if it were already so. We actually made plans to celebrate on the day we were debt free.

As with all demonstrations of a NEED, little breakthroughs showed up. We listed all of our debts from the highest interest debt to the lowest. Each month we eliminated another chunk of debt, celebrating our victories with a great home cooked meal. We went out very little. We rented movies and enjoyed putting our entertainment budget towards our debt free NEED!

I had another NEED that I did not tell Sherri about. I really NEEDED her to stop working where she was working. She is such a giver and doer that almost every week she would come home with another injury. She managed the Interior Division of a large greenhouse. As soon as my company could afford her salary I showed her all of the reasons that we would be better off if she traveled with me and helped me build a stronger company. It was an easy sale.

Within 12 months, we had only two remaining debts, our home mortgage and one vehicle payment. We had successfully paid off more than $100,000 of debt in one year! We had four years to go on our original 60-month plan. Admittedly, we had almost $200,000 more to go, however we had already accomplished what most people would call a miracle! We had another celebration dinner. I said, "I want to accelerate and build our debt free NEED even greater." Sherri said, "Steven, it seems to be working just fine. Look how far we have come in just 12 months." I said, "Yes I know, and I truly celebrate our achievements also; however, someday I will be teaching this NEED **success system** worldwide and most people will not BELIEVE me unless I have dramatic results to prove that this **success system** works!" That is when another Steven Lloyd-ism was born.

" If it doesn't work for you, don't export it!"

What I actually did without recognizing it at that time was to set yet another NEED into motion. I NEEDED to be able to prove to **you** that this **success system** works!

Sherri agreed. She said, "What do you have in mind?" I said, "I NEED for us to be 100% debt free in 12 months! The demonstrations that we have had so far have proven to me that the universal principles at work here have no time table except that which we BELIEVE in!" She said, "Okay, then I NEED it too!" We finished our dinner and did not discuss it for several days.

To add more fuel to our NEED fire, I set appointments on both our calendars for a mortgage burning party one year to the day that we set the new NEED into motion. Everything I said and did supported this new NEED BELIEF.

Three months went by and nothing had changed. Six months passed with no real economic change. Most people, with half of the time available to reach a goal being gone, would reevaluate the goal.

Instead, I reinforced my BELIEF system by rereading the stories like the one about the Chinese bamboo that, once planted, puts its roots down for five years before it even breaks the ground. Then, in just one year, it grows 20 feet! I resold both Sherri and myself that we were just like that bamboo tree!

Nine months passed. I had not discussed this debt free NEED with another living soul except my wife. I was on the road traveling, building the sales and marketing sides of the company. My business partner was running the administration and economic sides. I knew we had been reinvesting almost everything that we earned back into building the business. I also knew that most businesses do not show a profit for five years. We were just three years into the development of our company. One day while staying in yet another hotel room, my business partner called to say, "We NEED to have a serious economic conversation." My Heart sank. For the first time I saw my NEED moving away. When I returned to Dallas from my road trip, I went into the office to meet my business partner. I was prepared for the worst.

We moved our conversation to a small conference table in his office where he laid the company books out in front of me. He said, "We have or will have a serious tax problem very soon if we do not do something now." I said, "What do we need to do?" He said, "We need to distribute almost $500,000 dollars to the partners to avoid a serious double tax problem." I said, "We are the only two partners." He said, "Yea, I know, here is a check for your share!"

I was looking at a check that would pay off **all** my debts and put some extra money in our savings account! We had not only satisfied our NEED, we did it three months early!

As I looked at the check, I was speechless. Anyone who knows me well would tell you that my being speechless is a monumental event in and of itself. I called my mortgage company and asked for the total pay-off on the house. I asked them to prepare the settlement documents, went downstairs to the bank and deposited the check into my personal account. I got a bank draft for the entire payoff amount on the house. I drove to the Federal Express office myself to send off the overnight letter containing the bank draft and written request for mortgage payoff.

I left the office early to go home and show Sherri what I had done. I kept copies of everything. I opened the door and faked a real depressed look. She asked me what was wrong. I said, "I got some really intense news today!" She said, "What's the news?" I just handed her the big envelope of papers and let her discover the facts for herself. She sat down on the couch in my private office in our home and opened the envelope with real trepidation on her face. She looked at the photocopy of the check. She studied the copy of the bank draft and the letter to the mortgage company requesting mortgage payoff. She looked at me and said, "I don't understand, what is all of this?" I said, "This means we are debt free!" Twelve months from that date, our net worth was in excess of three million dollars.

If you are still squarely in your Chairperson's chair, then you probably have only one question running through your mind, and that question is, "How do I do the same thing for my life?"

The first step to helping you use this **success system** is to build your BELIEF system with so many demonstrations that this works, that your BELIEF system **automatically** overrides any thoughts, feelings, emotions, or BELIEFS to the contrary. You need to revisit your want list and pick one in each category that you BELIEVE you can attain or receive within 30 days. I am not starting with big tests because I want you to build such overwhelming positive evidence that you can hardly wait to get in front of one of my cameras to give your live testimonial on how well this **success system** works!

If you are in danger of losing your job or some other financially based possession that is important to you and that you NEED to keep, pick one of those. Weight loss or fitness NEEDS must be in line with what you know is smart and safe. Any weight loss NEED should never exceed three to five pounds per week. Any medical doctor will tell you that anything more aggressive than that is dangerous to your health. Like weight loss, physical fitness NEEDS must have demonstration dates that coincide with sanity.

All changes in your physical self NEED to be preceded by a good medical examination so that you know you are not putting any stress on any part of your body that is unhealthy. If you have or select emotional NEEDS and you have any history of emotional challenges, you NEED to consult your mental health care provider before you begin. You do not want to overwhelm yourself with huge changes that your mind or body is not ready to accept.

Also, if you are in a relationship with someone and that relationship is less than stable, have a meeting with him or her. You should **not** discuss the details of this plan with anyone for at least 63 days as I taught earlier. Not even your doctor NEEDS to know the details of what you are doing. You just NEED to know you are sound, fit, and in good medical health before you begin. Your relationship also NEEDS to be stable enough to allow you to receive your first few positive demonstrations. If it is not, you should resolve whatever issues exist between you first, so you are not pulled off your success track.

Normally, the following or a similar agreement is all that is NEEDED. Remember to sell them on the WIIFT (What's In It For **Them**).

Try this. "(Their name), I'm about to start a three-month professional growth and development program. It will require a major commitment of my time, focus, and energy. When I succeed, I will think, feel, and perform better. I will be able to give **you** more of the things that **you** want and need. Can you, and will you, support me for the next 90 days?"

Do not be surprised if they want to know details of what you are about to do. Remember your commitment; I do not want you to find out the truth the hard way. You NEED to keep your plan between you and me until you KNOW the right time to tell someone about your new success strategy. More often than not, well-meaning but ignorant friends, relatives, or business associates will often say things to discourage you from trying. Do not allow this to happen!

Now that you have all of your ducks in line and I have my legal beagles satisfied, let's get going so you can start enjoying the **having**, **doing**, and **being**. Before we start, raise your right hand and take the following pledge. Come on, you can read with your left hand! Raise your right hand and read **out loud**:

> *"I (state your name), promise and swear to make no major changes in my personal, professional, or economic relationships for at least the next 90 days!"*

The reason I had you take that pledge is simple. Starting now, you will feel, experience, and witness the EFFECTs of your inner power being increased dramatically. Until you give your brain a chance to become accustomed to the power, you may do something unwise like go buy a new home or divorce your spouse. Three months of using, enjoying, and working with your newly discovered power will allow your excitement and enhanced personal power to settle in. You will realize in three months that everything worth **having**, **doing**, or **being** is long term. Short-term wonders are a dime a dozen. By staying in your Chairperson's chair everyday, you will prevent your ego from taking over and spoiling everything you will demonstrate.

Remember that your ego is NOT your friend! It does not want you, the Chairperson, to succeed. When you do, and I mean succeed BIG TIME as the real YOU, you will see that you never needed your ego in the first place! So, keep doing your Chairperson exercise at least once a day when you get up in the morning. Repeat the Chairperson's process again if you start feeling weak, defeated, **or** too powerful.

During this entire process, you should not feel any more excited than a 12-year-old kid getting everything he's ever wanted. You should feel appropriately grateful for both your progress and for the people who are helping you get it.

Take out your NEED cards, the ones with the shortest-term timetable and look at the cards. Are all of the statements written in the *present* as a current NEED? If not, take new cards and rewrite them.

Take the three cards and look at each NEED. Now, vote on which one is the most important NEED and put that card in first place. Now look at all three cards again and vote for second place. Look at the cards and make absolutely sure you are looking at your first, second, and third most important short term NEEDS. Agreed? Good! Now, take cards number two and three and put them in a stack of two. Now, **tear them up into little pieces and throw away the pieces!**

I can just hear your brain screaming at me across time and space saying, "Oh Steven, it is so hard to do that because they have become NEEDS!" I understand. However, this is a very important part of this **success system** so, just do it! You will have a chance to work on those NEEDS as soon as you demonstrate the desired result for the one remaining NEED.

What you just did is to **triple** your NEED to attain the result behind your greatest NEED. Next, take out your calendar. Answer this question. How long, realistically, will it take you to achieve the satisfaction of this NEED? Look at your calendar and make your decision. Now, **cut that time frame in half!**

By now, you should really start to feel something taking form within you. This is your BELIEF **system** realigning itself and preparing to bring you the result behind your NEED. Take a deep relaxing breath and say these words out loud, *"Thank you, I accept!"* Come on, you can add more acceptance, gratitude, and enthusiasm than that! Try it again. Take a deep breath and shout out loud, **"THANK YOU, I ACCEPT!"** Good, this is exciting isn't it?

The next step we need to achieve is to build a clear mental equivalent of the desired result behind your NEED so that your brain knows exactly what it is going after. Open your notebook or journal and describe exactly what the achievement of your NEED looks like, sounds like, and feels like, in as much detail as possible. Add all of the colors, feelings, people, sounds, smells, and tastes. Paint this picture on paper with as much dimension and detail as possible.

Next, I know that this will seem redundant, but this is *very important.* Turn to a new sheet of paper and repeat this process again. This time, add in everything new that shows up in your mind. Now, take your notebook or journal and turn to yet a third sheet of clean paper. I want you to write a success statement describing the success demonstration of your NEED in 15 words or less. It would read something like; "I love the fact that I am the top producer in my office!"

Take a new 3x5 card and transfer those 15 or fewer words to the back of your 3x5 card. Write the following phrase on the front of the card. "I really, really, really NEED (your number one NEED). I need it as much as

I NEED to breathe! I am open to receive it now. I will do whatever it takes to have it now. Thank you, I accept it now!"

Well, do you have it yet? If not, it will not be long and you will. Carry this card with you along with your PMA card and read it with as much passion as that young man being held under the water had for NEEDING to breathe. As soon as it demonstrates, please write me and let me know all about it. I love reading success letters from my students. It's like a breath of fresh air for me to read about your achievements!

As soon as you receive what you NEED, celebrate your victory. Your brain NEEDS to feel the celebration dance. Take three days to rest and celebrate. Then, take the second NEED that you wrote on one of the cards that you tore up and repeat this process again. Remember to write out your 2nd, 3rd, and 4th NEEDS from your list. Pick your *new* **number one** NEED and tear up the other two. Keep receiving and celebrating the achievement of your NEEDS. Do not linger at the Success Plateau for more than three days. That is enough time for you to rest without setting up a camp that will, if you are not careful, become your new home. On the fourth day, start the climb again! If you will follow these instructions to the letter, you will be amazed and delighted at how wonderful your life and career will be in just one year! Here is another Steven Lloydism for you.

> "*Most people grossly exaggerate what is possible in a month. Those same people dramatically underestimate what is possible in just one year*"!

CHAPTER EIGHT

Intensifying Your
NEED

Do you recall the story of the young man being held under the water? Remember when he first laid back in the wise man's arms? He trusted that he would get what he sought, didn't he? He probably thought that he would magically get his answer. Like the young man, your answer and the attainment of your desired result is within you. Once your focus is as *crystal clear* on what it is that you NEED, just as clear as the young man's was for NEEDING to breathe, you will demonstrate your NEEDS with what appears to be speed, grace, and ease. Here is a Steven Lloyd-ism I want you to remember.

"*The secret to having, doing, and being, is in your knowing, not your doing. When you know what it is you NEED, you will know what it is you NEED to do!*"

How many times have you seen someone in complete and total despair with their head in their hands saying, "Oh, I don't know what I'm going to do?" Unfortunately, that scene is far too common. The solution, however, is NOT in the doing, it is in the KNOWING. What do you NEED to know? Your NEED is the answer!

The next secret in this **success system** is the tuning of your mental receiver. I am sure by now that you are feeling a surplus of emotional energy within you. I will also bet that your brain is still not clear on all of the details of how your desired result will be attained. Here again is where you NEED to trust me. You do not NEED to know HOW. Your job is to get completely clear on the WHY. There are two sides of the why: What you want and what you don't want.

Picture a football field in your mind. You are standing on the 50-yard line with a football. To your right is your goal, the arrival point where you win. To your left is your opponent's goal, the place or direction where you lose. This exercise will help you become very clear on all of the "moving towards," or where you want to go motivations, and all of the "moving away from," or where you don't want to go motivations. The game of football is a great metaphor because the game and its objectives are so easy to understand. If you run to the right far enough and fast enough, you win. If you go in the opposite direction, you lose. Your inner game works the same way.

I know that this may be completely new and may seem very complicated. It really is not anymore complex or difficult than any of the many accomplishments that you have already achieved.

Think back again to that same car in which you learned to drive. That experience seemed a little overwhelming at first too, didn't it? Imagine right now that you are sitting behind the wheel of that very first automobile. Look at all of the gauges, buttons, switches, dials, and pedals. Think about all of the minute variations and configurations necessary to have a smooth, safe, and successful transportation experience. What you are working on now is no more complex than learning how to drive a car, it is just different. If you can associate that same kind of new student driver excitement with what you are doing now, you will experience the same fun and excitement you felt then.

Please remember this new kid in school feeling. It is the *golden key* that will unlock your necessary compassion for the new kids you will help some day. We all have a tendency to be impatient with people trying to learn what we have already mastered. Remember this feeling of being new. If you hope to become a true Master, you will NEED this memory.

One of the greatest compliments I have ever received is that I seem to have the ability to take the complex and difficult and make it easy and fun to understand. I will let you be the judge of that. If I do that for you then my desired result will have been achieved. I do have a kind and compassionate Heart, because I can recall all of the times I was made to feel stupid, slow, or inept at doing something new that was hard for me, but easy for my instructor. What I have learned over the years, now that I am the teacher, is that my value as a teacher is measured by the percentage of my students that I really help.

I also measure my teaching success by how many people are able to do what I can do with ease, grace, and style while having fun doing it. This should be fun! After all, we are working on transforming every process of your life and career that CAUSE you pain, discomfort, sorrow, or failure, into automated **success systems** that will bring you happiness, pleasure, and success! Imagine how jazzed you will be to wake up every day KNOWING that you can have, do, or be **anything** you NEED.

Please do us both a favor and do not wake up one day with a very short list and blame anyone else for your lack of NEED fulfillment. Your wishes, wants, hopes, and dreams will NEVER come to you unless and until **you** build the foundation under them. That foundation is your burning NEED to have them, do them, and become them.

Once you have mastered this **success system**, do not be surprised if you become a little bored. Start now to dream **big dreams**. Even the Apollo Astronauts got depressed once they had their feet back on Earth. They did not have any other dreams to convert into NEEDS. Try to imagine working for years toward the goal of successfully going into and returning from outer space. Where do you go from there? Well, how about writing books, or doing lecture tours and corporate consulting for starters?

It is important that you know that any pain you experience in this acquisition process is in direct relationship to **your** resistance to doing the work and learning the lessons you NEED to do and learn. Once you stop resisting, you will stop experiencing pain.

This past summer I had my 12-year-old nephew Wesley come to stay with us for three weeks. He was supposed to stay for a month but he had to return one week early to get some tutoring on his schoolwork that he had left undone during his past year's classes. He was required by his mother to bring Spanish and reading assignments to catch up on while he was here. The amount of homework he had to do was in direct proportion to the work that he had left undone. We had a lot of fun, but nothing compared to the fun we could have had if he would have done the work when he was supposed to do it.

Life is like a loving parent or teacher. It does not care how many times you NEED or require the same lessons to learn and demonstrate that you KNOW. This is your rite of passage. Life really loves you just like a loving parent. If you are not ready to move up to the next grade, you will be held back until you are ready. This is NOT a punishment. Your pain of watching your classmates move on is **self-induced**. You can scream, holler, rant, and rave that "This is not fair!" Life does not really care because life, just like professional selling, is always 100% fair! You always get back in direct proportion to what you put in. Always remember that there is a huge difference between effort and effectiveness!

You can sit in front of an empty fireplace and say, "I will make you a deal, you give me heat and then I will give you wood." You will be cold for a very long time!

As much as you may want to reinvent the laws of physics, they are doing what all laws do. The laws of physics do not care if you understand or like them: they just keep working. You can get up on top of a building and jump off, and soon, very soon, you will notice that you are NOT heading Northeast! You are experiencing the Law of Gravity and you will experience all of the EFFECTS of its power. Do you really think that the Law of Gravity cares about your results or your pain? It cannot care, it is a law! It also functions in direct relationship to the way you use it. This is true of all of the other universal laws as well.

The Law of Compensation is the law at work in the lesson I am teaching you now. Your results will be in direct proportion to your understanding and application of this **success system**. The Law of Compensation says simply that what you put in must come back. When a gardener plants corn, he or she always gets corn. They never get wheat or oats or cabbage. Remember that the Law of Compensation does not stop at the planting. You must also follow through with the other critical requirements and steps. You must water, fertilize, weed, and care for your garden.

There are four basic human motivations. They are **love, greed, envy,** and **fear.** All four of these motivations can be used in a positive way to inspire you to move and keep moving toward your desired result. The secret to successful human engineering, at least from my perspective, is for you to KNOW that you are utilizing these emotions as motivators, not being controlled by them. When these motivations are used upon us, we feel manipulated. Even when you use them on yourself like a whip to drive yourself to achieve, you are not happy. You can be happy while you achieve. Contrary to what you have been taught to BELIEVE, the fear of failure does not CAUSE your success. The best that fear can do is to drive you to move and keep moving toward your desired result. Your applied skills, knowledge, and abilities CAUSE your success!

You may not consider yourself a runner, but you could be motivated to run farther and faster than you currently BELIEVE that you can run. If someone was running behind you with a buggy whip, whipping you every time you slowed down or stopped running, you would probably run faster and farther, true? Unfortunately, many sales managers use this very technique to "motivate" their salespeople. The best that they get is compliance. They never get what is possible when you enroll the Heart in the selling process!

What if I could show you a way to achieve World-Class performance results **and** to have all of the positive feelings, too? Well, I can do just that. Thousands of people are already accomplishing in just one year what most people work a lifetime to achieve. The best that most managers get is compliance jogging out of mandatory whipping! Most managers stand back in awe of someone who shows up with their running shoes on, ready, willing, and wanting to run.

These managers have not figured out the CAUSE, so they have manufactured a warehouse of explanations like "you have to be born with drive," or, "achievers are rare." Those explanations are utter nonsense! Every human being born is born with the seeds of greatness! Just look at what free enterprise has done in this country compared to any country that uses fear to control the behavior and expression of its people.

Without exception, when I have interviewed top performers in every field, they all knew WHY they NEEDED to perform at their World-Class level. Now, you will know, too. What you do with this knowledge is entirely up to you. My desire with this system is to show you that you, too, can be a World-Class performer. By helping you demonstrate small results, we will override any of your negative BELIEFS so that you KNOW beyond a shadow of any doubt that this **success system** works for you, too!

With each attainment of small and simple NEEDS, you will build a confidence and a KNOWING that this system will work for your big NEEDS, too. The secret is, make it easy to succeed and hard to fail!

I remember my high school archery class very well. The instructor put the targets 50 feet away. He taught us how to string a bow. He showed us how to string an arrow so that the two feathers that are flat go against the bow. He explained why we should wear the arm and shooting glove protection. Then, he had each of us try to hit the target. Nobody even hit the straw backing on the target! We all fell short of the target. Then he explained that we needed to aim high to, "arc our arrows into the target." On the second try, one girl aimed so high she shot the arrow 100 feet past the target and almost hit a kid on the running track! Even after weeks of trying, nobody ever hit a bullseye.

Years later, a friend of mine named Glenn wanted me to go bow hunting with him. He had been very successful at it. Guess what BELIEF I had about my ability to shoot a bow? You got it! I said, "I tried shooting a bow when I was in high school and, **I AM NOT GOOD AT IT!** Fortunately, Glenn learned how to shoot from a private instructor. He said, "That's utter nonsense. I will bet you that your high school PE teacher started your lessons with the target 50 feet or more away from you, didn't he?" I said, "How did you know that?" He said, "That doesn't matter. If you will set aside everything that you have been taught about shooting a bow, I promise to have you hitting the bullseye on your very first lesson." I agreed. I did not like having a BELIEF that I was a failure in any area of my life.

Glenn showed up at my Wisconsin country home with all of his bow and arrow equipment early the next Saturday morning. I was real excited about the possibility of mastering archery, but I still felt anxious. I still had a negative BELIEF about my bow shooting abilities.

Glenn went through a similar bow stringing, arm- and finger- protection lesson like the one I had received in high school. Because of the similarity of the lesson, my old BELIEF was firing off all kinds of emotions. I was starting to feel worse. When I was ready to shoot, Glenn had me place my back on the target and walk 10 feet away from it. He placed a stick on the ground to mark my starting point. He said, "Okay, hit the bullseye!" I said, "Anyone can hit it from here!" He said, "Exactly right.

Now shoot the bow and aim dead center at the bullseye!" I did as instructed. I hit the black of the bullseye, but not dead center. He said, "Do it again and this time aim just half an inch higher." I did as instructed and hit the bullseye, dead center, on my second try! "Wow," I said, "I get it. Make it hard to fail and easy to succeed, what a great idea!"

For the next hour my friend did exactly that. With every three successful bullseye hits, Glenn moved my stick back one foot at a time. He required that I stay at my new shooting position until I hit a bullseye at least three times in a row. By the end of my first lesson I was hitting the bullseye consistently from 50 feet away! With each success Glenn would say, "Good job" or, some other words of encouragement.

Isn't that what a loving parent does when we teach our kids to walk, talk, or do anything that is easy for us but new for them! We hold out our hands to catch them from falling as they take one successful step. Then we praise them for how well they did! Soon, very soon, they are running all over the house!

What do you suppose would happen if we had said to our toddler, "Okay, now that you've taken your first step, run out to the mailbox and bring back the mail? Also, don't forget to put all of the personal letters in one stack, all of the bills in another stack, and all of the junk mail in a third stack. And, while you're outside, please take out the garbage!" Then, when they fell down, we spanked them and called them bad and stupid! I suggest that we would have a whole society living in wheelchairs!

Has your personal and professional growth or sales training been much different? How much time, effort, and encouragement were invested in you to help you master what you see as difficult? Can you see and understand the relationship?

What if **you** had a Success Coach to take you by the hand and walk you through every single step of what you want to be great at, but currently are not? What if that coach went over and over every step again and again bragging on all of your victories and ignoring all of your failures? Well, that is exactly what I am doing for you now! Your inner greatness outweighs your shortcomings ten to one! Today, let us make success a habit in every area of your life. Agreed? Great!

Each of us is motivated by four basic human emotions. Again, they are, **love**, **greed**, **envy** and **fear**. Please take out your journal and rewrite your example NEED at the top of the page. You will also need to draw the following diagram in your journal.

You will revisit this chapter and this diagram several times to repeat this same process so it is best if this time you do **not** write in your book.

Love	Greed
Envy	Fear

Look at your NEED again. Our first desired result is to activate the power of *LOVE*. Ask yourself, "Who do I love enough to allow this NEED to be fulfilled?" As human beings we always seem to do more for someone else than we will do for ourselves. So let's use that knowledge to help and motivate ourselves toward what we want!

Answer this question: "What will I love about satisfying this NEED? What will I love seeing, feeling, and hearing about me when I satisfy this NEED?"

Next, we need to activate the *GREED* mechanism within you. What things will you get by satisfying your NEED? What status will you achieve by getting your NEED? What satisfaction will you get when your NEED is fulfilled?

ENVY can work for you too. Just answer the following questions. Who do I know that already has my NEED met? List all of the people!

Who do I know that makes my NEED appear easy? How will I feel about being accepted by these people once I achieve my NEED?

Lastly, we NEED to get *FEAR* working for you! We NEED to build the whip to drive you away from where you should not want to go. Here is where you NEED to make your negative, creative imagination work for you. Make these fears big, ugly, nasty, and mean! Answer these questions: What do I fear about not fulfilling my NEED? What bad thing or circumstance will happen or keep happening if I do not get my NEED? Who will I disappoint by not getting my NEED? What are all the losses I will experience by not finally doing what is necessary to get my NEED? Who will I hurt by not doing this work and not demonstrating this NEED?

Hopefully, you really put yourself into this process and felt the four basic emotions come alive! Your **creative imagination** and your **willingness** to make it real are the *golden keys* that unlock the doors between where you are and the attainment of your NEEDS.

The next secret to your lasting and automated success is locating and replacing the negative BELIEFS that are holding you back. Be sure you have at least one full hour of uninterrupted time before moving on to the next chapter. The benefits from the next chapter will amaze and delight you!

CHAPTER NINE

Negative BELIEF Replacement

Before you start this chapter, *please* be sure you have a **full hour** of uninterrupted time to work all the way through this segment. In this chapter we will be uncovering some of your negative BELIEFS. Each of these negative BELIEFS has strong negative emotions in them. It is critical that you have enough uninterrupted time to process them all!

Up until now you have probably felt very positive feelings from the work we have done. This chapter will expose other feelings that will come out of your negative BELIEFS. If you're not careful to work all the way through this chapter to the very end, you will have some negative BELIEFS kick your Chairperson out of your chair and you may indeed put this book down. It may take you days to get back into your chair and finish this work. So, please, work all the way through this chapter and do all the work so your own negative BELIEFS do not stop you.

Unlike most of the books on selling that you have read, and unlike all of the books you have read for entertainment or non-critical information, I have created this book more like a cookbook. You cannot and will not ever create a meal worth eating if you only read the recipes. If you want to create a life and a career worth having, you need to break some eggs, or, in this case, break some BELIEFS!

Now let's look inside your BELIEF system and discover a negative BELIEF that keeps you from having the life that you want and need. Take out your journal and turn to a new page. Call to mind a negative EFFECT you would like to change and write it down. It can be anything. This is a business book on selling, so why not pick an EFFECT that will increase your sales when it is changed? To help you identify the CAUSE I will repeat the four tests of a BELIEF that I have identified through my years of doing this work with hundreds of private clients.

They are:

1. When you speak the words that identify your belief, you feel an emotional energy.

2. You have a tendency to defend, explain, or justify your BELIEF.

3. The EFFECT or result tends to repeat itself over and over again.

4. When the BELIEF is expressed, it sounds or appears to be confusing to the observer but makes logical sense to the BELIEVER.

As I said earlier, you can choose any negative EFFECT or pattern that you NEED to change. You will enhance your sales career faster if you pick an effect that is preventing you from consistently performing at the level you want to achieve. Be bold and pick something big!

It may be helpful to give you a little background on what a negative BELIEF looks, sounds, and feels like from my own past. Through this example you will see the CAUSE and EFFECT relationship. You will also see the immediate benefit that is available to you.

In 1992, I was sitting in a hot tub relaxing after a long day. I was pondering an EFFECT that was holding me back from growing my private practice and speaking business. I noticed that the EFFECT was that I would do anything to avoid making promotional telephone calls. I could no longer avoid the FACT that I had a negative BELIEF about using the telephone for business.

It is common for the BELIEF or its result to not make logical sense. I was confused and unsure that it was a BELIEF because I loved to talk on the telephone for all of the other reasons except business! I often used the telephone to talk to friends and relatives to avoid using the telephone for business. I was in a BELIEF box, and I knew it!

As I contemplated my situation, which is the first step of self-improvement, I had this age-old thought cross my mind, "Physician heal thyself." So, I did. I had used my techniques to help all of my clients but I had never used a Belief Replacement Training (BRT) process on myself. I was not really sure if I could use it on myself. I knew I had nothing to lose and a lot to gain if it worked. I created a Coach character in my mind so I could play the role of the client. I gave the Coach permission to create a new and unique process. It not only worked, but I got a brand new technique to use with my advanced clients! That was also the day that the term, BELIEF Replacement Coach (BRC) was born!

The science of BRT demonstrates a consistent result that proves the process is indeed successful. In both math and science it is called "proving your theory." BRT stands for Belief Replacement Training. Training is done in a group, in a live workshop, on film, or even audiocassette tape. Belief replacement coaching is normally done one on one.

The human mind is both complex and simple. It is complex in that its capacity and ability is enormous, if not unlimited. It is simple in that the mind can and does operate on predictable patterns, with predictable results, much like a computer.

The computer is more than a metaphor for the human mind. Remember that the human mind created the computer. Therefore the production of the computer, as limited as it may be, gives us great insight into how our human mind works. It also gives us a system to duplicate, CAUSING all predictable changes in our own thinking.

Regardless of your computer knowledge, what happens if you go to the DOS root directory, find a Windows98 program, type in an erase command, and then press "enter?" Well, you get one more chance to change your mind. You will see a small question at the bottom of your screen that says "Are you sure?" If you type in "yes" and press the enter key, GONE! As difficult as it may be for you to BELIEVE, this example illustrates that programs can also be erased from your own human computer through BRT.

The Windows98 program code still exists, even though our perception is that it was fully erased. Your brain works in a similar manner.

If this were not true, why is it that someone who has smoked for twenty years and tried everything to stop suddenly quits cold turkey one day and never smokes again? If you follow the brain code change backwards, you will find the answer.

Normally when someone tries to stop smoking, the code BELIEF that gets activated says, "If I don't stop smoking, I will experience less pain than the fear of smoking." Result, the program change is **incomplete**.

Then, one day, this person meets someone who rewrites the program. The new code says, "If I don't stop smoking, I will feel the awful pain of trying to breathe, compared to the little discomfort I may feel by stopping smoking!" And, "Bing," **gone**! New program **complete**. New demonstration is complete!

There was a TV episode of *ER* where Dr. Mark Green was really struggling with quitting smoking. He had all of the intellectual knowledge as to why he should stop smoking. His other doctor friends and colleagues all harassed him about smoking. Nothing worked until a programmer in the form of a cancer patient just happened to come under his care. Not only could Dr. Green not cure this man, he could not even lessen his pain.

The scene where the programming actually took place was when Dr. Green found the cancer patient on the floor, dead from a self-inflicted gunshot wound. This man could no longer endure the pain and agony of trying to breathe. This man could no longer take the pain of watching his dear wife suffer as she stood helpless and watched him struggle just to breathe! Remember that BELIEF replacement is **not** an intellectual process, it is an **emotional experience**! The next scene showed Dr. Green dumping his cigarettes in the toilet. He flushed them out of his life, once and for all. "Bing," new program **complete**. New demonstration **complete**! Like hundreds of my BRC clients, he never smoked again.

You are probably saying, "Come on Steven, it can't be that simple!" Oh, yes it is, but, it is not easy! Remember, easy indicates little effort and little or no pain.

The code in your brain has basic binary configurations. The top polar configuration is pleasure and the bottom polar configuration is pain. Think of your brain like a cow standing behind an electric fence. You are enjoying what room you have as it is defined by your pleasure and the pleasure is defined as your avoidance of the painful electric fence.

When I was a kid on our Wisconsin farm, we raised a herd of beef feeder cattle each year for additional income. Beef cows are difficult to keep contained. One day my dad brought home the latest new electric fence transformer called, The Weed Burner.

One of the challenges with electric fences is that the weeds grow up, touch the electric wire, and ground it. This renders the fence impotent and useless. This new transformer sent four times the normal voltage and amperage through the wire. It had a very short pulse because it not only takes a very short burst of pain to teach a cow to stay away, but anything longer could stop even a full grown cow's heart, not to mention a human being. The blast of electricity was so strong that it would burn the weeds off of the wire; thus, the name, Weed Burner.

One warm, moonlit night, I was in the barn doing chores with my mother and I needed to take a break. I went outside to get some fresh Wisconsin air. There I was enjoying the sounds of the crickets harmonizing with the choir of bullfrogs. I remember staring up at a nearly full moon and enjoying my little walk when all of a sudden, "WHAM!" I found myself on the ground, feeling the worst pain of my 12 years of life! I had walked into the electric fence!

The point of the story is that I never went anywhere near that electric fence, or any fence, again! I had a whole new "Fence BELIEF." Even to this day, I approach all fences with that memory still in my mind. I leave the BELIEF in place, because it keeps me safe.

Look again at the one negative EFFECT you want to change and find the PAIN/CAUSE where your BELIEF was installed. What was the point of impact? There is always a frozen moment in time for all of us where the motivation was so strong, we were changed from that moment forward. Remember my fear of the phone problem? Here is what CAUSED it:

My two sisters—Cherrie and Carla—and my brother Bill and I were raised on a farm just outside a small rural community called Rice Lake, Wisconsin. Now, I know that there are a lot of other authors that claim to be from Rice Lake, Wisconsin but I really am from Rice Lake! I mention this only because when you read the story, if I did not explain that technology always finds its way to the small corners of our country last, you would think I am 94 years old!

The telephone service that was provided to us on this small farm was a party line. Our farm shared the same line as several of our neighbors. My older brother Bill found what he thought was a great way to make "free" long distance calls. He would dial "0" and give the operator the number he wanted to call, and then when she would ask for our number, he would give her someone else's telephone number. He thought he was being really smart and creative.

Our stepfather was a man of European descent who was known for his temper. It took a long while for the telephone company to trace down all of those illegal telephone calls. I remember this event as if it were yesterday. One Saturday morning we were all sitting in the kitchen having breakfast following our morning chores. Dad walked into the room with some papers in his hand and a look on his face that looked like we had just lost the farm. He threw the papers in front of my brother and screamed, "What in the world do you think you're doing?"

He made my brother Bill read the letter out loud. It was very strong! It threatened to cut off our telephone service. When you live miles from the nearest town, telephone service is critical. The company demanded immediate payment. In today's economic equivalent it would translate to over one thousand dollars! My dad grabbed the back of my brother's chair and dragged him across the kitchen floor to the wall phone. This was the point of impact for me. Remember that a BELIEF will take root—or install—at a moment of intensity when the human mind is affected by an intense experience. This can be pain, fear, or pleasure.

Our stepfather was in a rage. The veins were sticking out of his head and neck. He grabbed the phone from the cradle and shook it up and down like a hammer, as if he was going to hit my brother with it. He kept repeating, *"The phone is not for fun, the phone is for business, the phone is not for fun, the phone is for business!"*

I did not realize how that frozen moment in time impacted my business life as far as the telephone was concerned. Just to finish the story for you, my dad did not hit my brother with the phone. Bill was never allowed to use the phone again and he had to move into the chicken coop where he lived for seven years (I'm joking)! He did, however, have to work long and hard to pay off that phone bill.

Look again at the phrase, *"The phone is not for fun, the phone is for business."*

My observation and personal experience is that the mind absorbs only the verbs and nouns. Words like not, don't, won't, shouldn't, couldn't, wasn't, doesn't, or isn't actually tell your brain to do exactly the opposite of what you want. The verb and nouns go directly into the subconscious mind as an order! Also, when the brain associates pain with a positive noun or verb, it normally does the exact opposite.

If you are experiencing or observing results you do not want from yourself or others, listen to the words you use and the order in which you use them. See if you have a history of telling yourself or others what you do **not** want instead of what you **do** want. **Not** is an adverb. It is never used as a verb in either our speech or our thoughts. The adverb **not** expresses an idea which is the exact opposite of the regular meaning of the verb. Ask any English professor and they will tell you that this is true. Ask any parent what happens when they tell their children, "Don't play in the street!" Guess who they find playing in the street when they get home? Try telling people, and yourself, what behavior you do want. Imagine the benefits of saying to your child, "Stay in the yard!" Why would you ever tell them or anyone else including yourself, what you do **not** want them to do? The order that goes into their subconscious mind is, "Play in the street!" This is one of the many things that has amazed me about the study of the human mind and our BELIEF system and our behavior. One of my students reported to me that this one lesson has been one of the most productive she has ever learned. She said, "I had no idea that I was the one telling myself to do what I did not want myself to do."

There is a story about Warren Spahn, the famous pitcher for the (then) Milwaukee Braves. He was in the bottom of the ninth inning with the bases loaded and the count was three and two. The Braves were ahead by one run. Except for a foul ball, he was about to pitch the last pitch of the game. His manager called for a time out, walked out to the mound and said, "What ever you do, don't throw the ball low and outside!" Guess where he threw the ball? You guessed it, low and outside! Warren walked over to the dugout after losing the game and said to his manager, "Why would you ever tell anyone what you **don't** want them to do?" Look at all the options the manager had. If he really knew what the batter could and would most likely hit, then he also knew what pitch the batter was most likely to miss, right? Try telling yourself and others exactly what you want.

Each person makes a unique association, even with the same experience. The BELIEF I linked up was, *"The phone IS for fun and NOT for business."* I associated pain in the energy form of fear to business and the order that went into my mind was, "Is for fun" because my brain, like your brain, responds best to the verb and the noun. Our brains tend to ignore the adjective and the adverb. Years later when I asked my brother Bill what impact that event had on him, he could hardly recall it. He said, "Yes, I remember doing something with the phone that got me into a little trouble." I said, "A little trouble?" All of those years I was harboring a negative BELIEF about the phone and he could hardly recall the event!

Now here is where the confusion **and** the secret lie. I linked up a BELIEF that released an energy called emotion that said, "The phone and business equals pain!" Remember that logic plays no role in emotion! How many times have you heard someone in an emotional state of mind saying things that make no logical sense? How many times have you expressed an emotion that your logical mind said, "This makes no sense?" Hopefully, by now you are at least starting to see that this undesirable EFFECT is a program called a BELIEF.

Here are the 12 steps for BELIEF replacement. This process will help you discover the moment of impact where the BELIEF was installed.

1. Write down the EFFECT that you want to change.

2. Relax your mind and think only of the EFFECT.

3. Follow the EFFECT from where you are to each of the times it has shown up in your life.

4. Follow the EFFECT in reverse, all the way back to the very first time it appeared.

5. Go back in your memory to a time before the EFFECT showed up.

6. Come forward again to the first time it appeared.

7. Ask yourself, "What are the emotional events surrounding the time I first made this mental association?"

8. What phrases did you hear or emotions did you experience or thoughts did you think at that moment?

9. What feelings, thoughts, or emotions are you experiencing today?

10. Write down the words about the BELIEF just as they showed up.

11. Use the words or phrases to create a label to identify this BELIEF.

12. Notice if your mind reacts as you recite out loud the words that label your BELIEF. Do you notice at least one of the four tests? If you do, you have found a BELIEF.

Again, the four tests are:

1. When you speak the words that identify your BELIEF, you feel emotional energy.

2. You have a tendency to defend, explain, or justify your BELIEF.

3. The EFFECT or result tends to repeat itself over and over again.

4. When the BELIEF is expressed, it sounds or appears to be confusing to the observer but makes logical sense to the BELIEVER.

The letters BRT represent different things depending on how they are used. The "B" always stands for "BELIEF." The "R" can represent "Release" or "Replacement," depending on which process we are using to change the BELIEF. The "T" represents "Training." The training is done in workshops, with video tape, or using audiocassette tapes. I have also done highly effective BRT in groups of hundreds. I have even done BRT on the telephone with great results! I have a certified BRC Coach program for people who want to help others as well as themselves. Many of my students have done very successful BRT and BRC sessions on themselves and with others. Everyone has "stuff," BRT and BRC is the fastest and most effective way I have found to release and replace it. The magnificent results speak for themselves. (If you want to learn more, see the Resources Section in the back of this book.)

I will teach you two techniques. The first requires you to use your creative imagination and your emotions again. Please know that this will not work if you are **not** going to use your creative imagination **and** your emotions. Also, if you allow your logic to try to define this process, your results will not be acceptable! Remember that a BELIEF is **not** a logical issue, it is an emotional experience. To get the BELIEF to release, we must use an equal or greater energy than was used to install it.

Before we begin, let me repeat that it is **critical** that you **not** be interrupted during this process. If there is any chance that you will not have 30 minutes to finish what you are about to start, please stop reading until you do have the time. Make sure that phones, pagers, or other possible distractions are turned off.

Before we replace your BELIEF program, you need to design a new BELIEF program to install in its place. Look at your negative BELIEF and let's design a new positive BELIEF to replace it. When we are finished with this exercise, you will feel great. Your new positive BELIEF statement must be short, powerful, and easy for your brain to accept. Let me give you an example of my new positive BELIEF about the phone.

"The phone is for fun AND for business!"

Now, write **your** new positive BELIEF.

To associate pain with your negative BELIEF, you must be willing to see, hear, and feel all of the horrible things that will happen to you, your loved ones, and your career if your negative BELIEF does not release.

Trust me, you must experience **real pain** and associate that pain with the negative BELIEF for it to release. You will feel it when it releases. The feeling is similar to the relief experienced when you remove a splinter. The pain of digging it out is really intense, but when it is out, there is a genuine sense of BELIEF RELIEF. I refer to it as wrapping barbed wire around the BELIEF and pulling it out. When your brain experiences the pain and you associate that pain with the BELIEF, your brain will release it! Again, BELIEF RELIEF!

As soon as you feel the shift of the release, you NEED to start the positive BELIEF installation process **immediately**. It is **critical** that you start the installation process of the positive BELIEF **immediately** following the release of your negative BELIEF. If you do not, the next intense event that your brain experiences will install where the old BELIEF was. Think of it like digging out a big weed in the garden of your mind. As soon as you get the weed out, you need to plant what you want in the very same spot, or another weed will take root!

The following is a process I have used successfully many times. Imagine you are walking down an old set of railroad tracks. It is a warm summer's day. Look down and see the railroad ties and the gravel between them. Look ahead from where you are walking. See an old fashioned train sitting at the railroad station. See the kind of train that you've seen many times in the old western movies.

As you approach the station, you see the old black engine, the coal car, and an open-air car with bench seats all facing forward towards the engine. Standing on the dock of the station is a character that represents your negative BELIEF. Make this character anyone you want. Notice all of the details of this character and how those details relate to the details of your negative BELIEF.

Walk over to the dock and take your character by the hand, help him down the steps of the dock, and walk him over to the open-air car. Help your negative BELIEF character up into the car and ask him to sit down in the first bench seat.

Get on the same car and face your negative BELIEF character. Allow me to speak these words through you, to your negative BELIEF. "What you are about to experience is what our life is going to look like if you do not get off the train and out of my life at the end of this ride. I know you came along to help and protect me from pain but I have outgrown any need for you. You are now CAUSING me the very pain that you were trying to protect me from."

Hang on to the handrail of the car and feel your body being jerked forward by the locomotive into the future. As the train picks up speed, see yourself moving year after year into the future with this negative BELIEF still controlling your life! See the scenes, feel the pain, make it real and intense, and associate this pain with the negative BELIEF! What do your personal, professional, and financial lives look like five years from now, better or worse? Associate the pain with the CAUSE. It is your negative BELIEF that is controlling you and causing the pain. Now, make the pictures, feelings, emotions, and results even more intense, nasty, and painful! See yourself ten years into the future. Do you still have any of your friends, family, or business associates still putting up with the behavior that is being CAUSED by this negative BELIEF? Say, "NO!" See yourself alone and lonely. See yourself digging through dumpsters for food! Make the pictures big, colorful, nasty, and mean! Associate the pain with this negative BELIEF! This is what is CAUSING the pain!

See yourself and the train pulling into a beautiful country meadow. Feel the train coming to a slow, easy stop. A few feet from you is a park bench with an old-fashioned broom, the round kind that they used to clean houses in the old west, leaning against the park bench. There is a concrete landing for you to step down onto that runs down a gentle slope to a large round concrete circle. You see a golden beam of light coming down out of the heavens to the very center of the round concrete circle. You hear the most beautiful celestial music you've ever heard. It's like the voices of angels singing. It is so wonderful, peaceful, and relaxing.

Step down from the train, look up at your negative BELIEF character and ask, "Are you ready to return to the loving place from which you came?" See your character nod, "Yes." Extend your hand and help him down from the train. Walk your negative BELIEF down the hill to the center of the circle and help him step into the golden light. Watch as your negative BELIEF is pulled up, up, up into the light. See him rising up, up, up out of your mind, body, and memory, back to where he came from. Wave goodbye to him and feel him completely leave you. Say out loud, "Goodbye," and see and feel him going, farther and farther away. See him getting very small as it floats higher and higher, going, going, GONE!

Walk over to the bench near the train and pick up the old broom. Take it into the car where your negative BELIEF sat and sweep every corner of the car. Sweep out all of the old dust memories of ever having that negative BELIEF in your mind and life. Sweep out all of the cobwebs of feelings, all of the dirt of emotions, all of the scraps of feelings left behind by that negative BELIEF. Sweep your mind clean of every thought, feeling, memory, and emotion that is associated with that negative BELIEF.

Notice a gentle rain starting to fall. Feel it wash you clean of every thought, feeling, memory, and emotion of that negative BELIEF. See this rain wash your open-air car clean of whatever remnants are still left behind of that negative BELIEF. See pure, clean water as it picks up all of the old dust, cobwebs, and trash and washes it out of the car, down the hill, and into the golden light. See it all being sucked up into the turning and spinning golden light, like a mini-tornado, up, up, up into the light. Watch it as it rises up out of your mind, life, and memory, completely and forever! Watch it as it leaves and moves farther and farther away until you can no longer see it. It is gone!

Notice that the rain has stopped and the sun is shining warmly on your face. Take a deep, cleansing breath and hear the birds chirping in the trees. Slowly release the breath and feel the newness of your freedom. Feel a giant smile coming across your face. Feel the joy and excitement as it fills you with power and passion. Feel the joy and excitement expand as you know that you're about to install a new, positive, and empowering BELIEF that will draw and lead you into a life that you have only dreamed possible. **Let yourself get excited!**

Get down from the open-air car you are in and walk up to the engine. Look up at the Engineer. See him smiling at you. Somehow, someway, you know that you know him. He is very familiar to you. See him extend his hand to help you up into the cab of the engine. Take his hand and step up into the engine cab.

Look ahead of you. There is a track to the left to take you back to your past failures and old way of living and a track to the right to take you to your new life. Turn to the engineer and say, "Take the right track!"

Feel your insides, jumping with excitement and joy as you feel the locomotive lunge forward! Feel your inner power build with confidence as you feel the locomotive increase speed.

As you feel the speed increasing, you hear the "puff, puff, puff, puff" of the engine moving faster and faster. As you look out of the window, you see yourself moving up this long gentle incline. As you crest the top of the hill, you see a huge paper banner across the tracks. As you steam closer and closer and faster and faster, you read the words of your new positive BELIEF statement on the banner. You are moving faster and faster and faster toward it. The engineer turns to you and says, "Is this what you really want? After we break through it, you will have it installed!" You turn to the engineer and say, "Oh yes, please go faster, I want it so much!" The engineer pushes full speed ahead and you feel the train increase speed even more as you are moving faster and faster and faster toward your new dream BELIEF.

Now, you are only a few feet from it. There it is: your new, powerful, positive BELIEF! As you suddenly break through, you see, feel, and hear things differently. Everything is clearer. You are completely relaxed. You are completely at peace and are very calm. You know you are now travelling at the speed of Positronic BELIEF!

Even though you know you are moving very fast, everything seems slower, easier, and you feel happy and full of joy!

The engineer smiles at you and says, "I knew you would love this! I am so proud of you for taking this trip. What you are about to see is what your life will look like if you will just follow the easy, simple, basic instructions for developing your new positive BELIEF."

See your life five years into the future with your new positive BELIEF, automatically attracting all of the people, things, and opportunities. Feel humble and proud of what you can now do. See how your new positive BELIEF creates such value for the people that you care about.

See an office door with your new professional title on it. Feel, accept, and BELIEVE it because this is your future! Clap your hands and say these words out loud, "**THANK YOU, I ACCEPT!**" Clap your hands harder and say the words louder! "**THANK YOU, I ACCEPT!**"

Well, that was interesting and fun, wasn't it? Don't you feel much better after just a few hundred words? If you really enrolled in the process, you just answered, "Yes!" Well, what CAUSED it? Was it the paper or ink? Was it your chair? Well, come on, what was it? I understand this process is obviously more intense, real, and powerful in a live workshop, or on film or even audiocassette tape. However, at some level, depending on how well you allowed yourself to participate in this exercise, you had some type of an experience. It is not easy for me to relay this to you with just the written word. You can probably now see why people have me coach them personally or to train their entire organization through these different dimensions. However, by just using the printed version of this process, you are now different at some level.

Your job now is to collect hundreds of pieces of evidence to reinforce and help your new positive BELIEF to grow. It needs to take root deeply in your subconscious mind. The following Positronic Mind Affirmation will help you do just that. Copy it down on a 3x5 card and read it with deep emotion. Just like the others I have already given you and that you must keep using, read it out loud first thing after waking up, before your noon meal, and again just before you go to sleep at night.

Carry your personal journal with you everywhere. It is crucial for you to write down all of the things you notice that verify that your new personal positive BELIEF is real and works regardless how small or insignificant you think it is. Remember to mark today as your start date and your end date 21 days in the future. You need a minimum of 21 days of positive BELIEF integration time.

If this new positive BELIEF is important to you and you want it to serve you for a long time, then you need to continue this process and develop it for the two additional periods of 21 days (63 days). If you do, this new program can very well be permanent! It is **your** life and career; you decide. The following Positronic Mind Affirmation will help you accomplish building this new positive BELIEF into the powerful program you need to help you to take **your** life and career into **your** next Dynamic Dimension. As before, write out the following PMA on a 3x5 card.

Fill in your new positive BELIEF where I have indicated. Follow the same morning, noon, and night (MNN) format as taught earlier.

Here is your PMA

My life and mind are now connected to a greater POWER than ever before. My new personal BELIEF of (fill in your new positive BELIEF) is growing, taking root, and serving me now. I see its power everywhere. I feel it filling old, empty spaces. There is no power or value in thoughts, feelings, or BELIEFs contrary to my new personal BELIEF. This is now the law of my life and I live it in love, gratitude, and humility. Thank you, I accept! And so I BELIEVE and so I achieve, and so it is!

The next step on your success journey is to open your mind to what you really want. Keep reading. The results from the next chapter will amaze and delight you.

CHAPTER TEN
BELIEF Release Training

OPENING YOUR MIND TO WHAT YOU REALLY WANT

I promised you two techniques for changing your BELIEFS, so here is the second technique. To allow this to work the way I designed it, you will need four small pieces of paper. Any type of paper will do just fine.

As with all of my lessons, the requirements emerged from years of testing and proving that these techniques, processes, and **success systems** deliver proven results. The successful results I know you will achieve by following each recipe as designed and outlined are verified by the many people who have achieved major breakthroughs in their personal, professional, and financial lives. Please follow each step as closely as you can and you will get similar positive and powerful results.

I want you to associate a great deal of success and pleasure with this process. Therefore, I will start slow, easy, and gradually. Hitting the bulls-eye early in your training will help build the self-confidence that you will need to tackle the really tough issues that keep pulling you back like a bungy cord that stops you just short of your desired result!

This next process is far subtler than the first. Most people need to work with this BELIEF Release Training technique several times to see and feel a significant change. This is, however, a little like sanding a knot or blemish off of your life versus cutting it out using the other BRT technique. This is however an extremely useful and powerful tool. One of the many things my students love about this technique is that it is portable and available to you anytime and anywhere you need it.

Mastering this and the other form of BRT are the *golden keys* that will unlock the door to your Emotional Buying Center (EBC). Once **your** Heart is open and free of pain, anger, resentment, and agendas, other people's Hearts will fly open to you, too.

Heart Selling will seem easy once you do the work within yourself that allows others to feel safe letting you in. You do not CAUSE other people's walls or defenses; your stuff just triggers or reinforces them.

The following BRT technique can be used anytime you feel some emotion or energy within you. When you *Sell From The Heart,* you will see, feel, and hear other people being drawn to you. As you process, release, and replace more and more of your negative BELIEFS and strengthen your positive BELIEFS, a magnetic type of energy actually draws people and opportunities to you. This energy is what explains the phenomenon called charisma.

If you listen to people try to explain why they are **not** charismatic, you will hear pure nonsense like, "Well, I'm not charismatic because, blah, blah, blah." Many people will say, "Charisma is a gift, so, very few have it, most others do not!" You will also hear other people say, "I could be charismatic but, blah, blah, blah." All of those "blah, blahs" are rationalizations and utter nonsense, nothing more and nothing less. They are incorrect descriptions of walls and blocks, which are BELIEFS that these people BELIEVE keep them safe. Those same programs keep them from shining the Heart light that draws others in like weary wanderers on the prairie, into a warm and inviting campfire on a dark cold night.

The warmth from others that we call charisma is nothing more and nothing less than positive energy emanating from their EBC or Heart. The great news is, like *Heart Selling*, it is a talent, skill, and ability that can be learned. You have the ability and you can experience the results if you first rid yourself of the "stuff" blocking the real you. Getting and staying open and clear cannot be manufactured or faked. You will see for yourself that the more open and clear you are, the more open and clear you must stay. When you start to hide again, you can feel that other people sense you hiding. This will happen during your progress toward true *Heart Selling*. They in turn hide or withdraw from you. Just notice it and go back and follow the recipes I have outlined in this book and you will release and replace whatever is blocking you. You will regain your openness and see and feel other people drawn to you once again.

We all have four base human emotional NEEDS or CAUSE motivations that support our lives like the Four Corners of any solid building foundation. They are, **control, security, approval,** and **acceptance.** Earlier I said that we have four basic human emotional expressions. They are, **love, greed, envy,** and **fear.** As real as these appear to be, you can trace each one back to one or more of these four root NEED CAUSES within your human experience.

Think of **control, security, approval,** and **acceptance** as the four main foundational legs that support your entire BELIEF system. Remember, what you focus on develops your thoughts. Your thoughts expand into feelings. Your feelings develop into your emotions. Your emotions create your BELIEFS. Your BELIEFS control how you act, react, or interact with people and life in general. Please keep in mind that this formula of BELIEF development also works in reverse. Your BELIEFS will trigger your emotions that stimulate your feelings that affect your thinking that will change your focus!

Let's apply scientific reason and see if each one of the four emotional expressions can be traced to one or more of their four foundational CAUSES. First, let's examine **greed.** If you will do your research, you will see the same one-to-four relationship I found in **control, security, approval,** and **acceptance.** After all, what is greed? Greed is a NEED for control! Greed is also a BELIEF of lack of control that drives one to hoard. It is also a NEED to feel secure by amassing vastly more things or money than a person could ever use. A good case could be made for greed being CAUSED by a lack of **approval** and **acceptance,** as well.

How about the emotion called **envy?** What are those who experience envy, envious of ? Could it possibly be **control, security, approval,** and **acceptance?** Interesting isn't it? The answer, of course, depends upon the person who is envious. The emotion of envy is, generally speaking, a BELIEF in the lack of **control, security, approval, or acceptance.** The person who is envious wants what someone else has but they BELIEVE they do not have it, or never will have it, or they would not be envious. Why would you have envy for what you BELIEVE you could have or could have if you wanted or needed it? Scientific reasoning would say that you would not. You do not envy what you already have or are in the process of obtaining!

Next, examine **love**. What is love? Noah Webster, in his original unabridged dictionary, stopped after many tries to define the word love. There is a great old joke about Mr. Webster. It was said of him that he was a true pragmatist. He was exacting in his thinking and use of words. The joke is that his wife caught him kissing their maid. She said, "Noah, I'm surprised!" Mr. Webster said, "No dear, I'm surprised, you are astonished!"

Webster's **love** definitions run the gamut from, "Warm affectionate feelings for," all the way to just this side of his definition for the word "lust."

If you put each of his definitions under the four "microscopes" of **control**, **security**, **approval**, and **acceptance**, I am confident that you too will find that the emotion of love falls under a need for at least one of them. Admittedly you must be willing, in some cases, to look at the broadest definitions of each and to understand that these base foundational CAUSES of human action and reaction are not necessarily a need for our personal **control, security, approval,** and **acceptance**. In the case of love, it could be a need for us to know that someone we love is accepted, approved of, has security, and is demonstrating control of his or her life. How else would you explain our desire or NEED for someone else's happiness?

True love for someone else CAUSES our need to know that they are happy, safe, and prospering, true? At some level we know someone we love cannot be truly happy if his or her life or relationships are out of control, correct? This understanding is what drives **your** feelings. The other person may be in some hypnotic trance BELIEVING that they are just fine, when in fact they are not. The BELIEFS that drive most addictive compulsive behaviors are what CAUSE people to think they are in control, when the reality is that their life is out of their control.

Would you agree that someone you love could not be truly happy if they have no form of security? Would you also agree that happiness is not possible without feelings of approval and acceptance? How can you be happy if you feel unapproved of or unaccepted?

I BELIEVE the secret to true happiness is reaching the Dynamic Dimension where we are able to find all of these qualities within ourselves. It is not only possible, it is critical that we discover, develop, and pursue our own inner powers of **control, security, approval,** and **acceptance.** Once we build these qualities within us, the outer demonstrations of "things" will appear to rise to the level and degree that we BELIEVE they are NEEDED!

Follow me to examine the most used and abused of all human emotions, **fear**! What is fear really? In its mildest form it appears as discomfort or as an uncomfortable feeling. In its grandest expression it shows up as a debilitating, disabling form of human trauma requiring restraint, protection, and medication.

Tune in and adjust your microscopes of **control, security, approval,** and **acceptance.** Examine any form of fear you like. In its most intense state, fear is an enormous BELIEF of a lack of **control, security, approval,** and or **acceptance.** In its mildest form, fear shows up as a NEED for them.

If you invest the thousands of hours of research that I have and really examine each and every feeling you and others experience, you will, I trust, come to the same or similar conclusions I have. If you notice any resistance within yourself right now, look inside and see if it is coming from a BELIEF that says, "It can't be that simple!" I too struggled with that BELIEF for a long time until I realized my BELIEF also fell into the same four base emotional CAUSE motivations of **control, security, approval, and acceptance.** It really is just that simple!

Yes, this process is as **simple** and **effective** as I have described. However, it is not easy. As I have explained with the other secrets I have already shared with you, effort and work are required if you want to reach the desired results that you say you want and need. The great news is that these processes will actually require far less work and far less pain than is required for you to maintain your current levels of resistance. They also require far less time and money than other forms of internal change.

The ease, joy, passion, and benefits of being free of your stuff are right now before your eyes. I suggest that you have known this was possible all along. The proof is in the fact that you bought or somehow obtained this book! If you did not BELIEVE that there really was a better, faster and more efficient **success system** to get you where you want and need to be, why are you still looking to find it? It is widely agreed that we only look for something that we really BELIEVE exists. Keep reading and you will find it! It is also common to resist your own discovery when you first find it. Think about when you first discovered something else that you tried to accomplish and found that it really worked. Think back to that last really great system you used: how stunned you were at how easily and effectively that it worked.

I truly do understand any feelings you may have about this book being too good to be true. I, too, had similar feelings when I first discovered this technique. If you think carefully about what I am about to say, it will make perfect sense to you. You can only become the recipient of the benefits, and therefore become a true BELIEVER, *after* you do the work and get the desired results! It is not possible to receive the benefits unless you trust and follow the process. You truly have nothing to lose, and World-Class personal, professional, and financial results to gain. You are going to love the benefits of this BRT technique, so let's begin!

To feel the subtle benefits of this technique, it is really helpful if you use four small pieces of paper. Write the word, "control" on one piece of paper, "security" on the next one, "approval" on the third, and "acceptance" on the last one.

The next step is critical to your success with this process. The hand with which you squeeze your piece of paper needs to be your **non-dominant** hand. You'll understand why when you get to the chapter on brain language. For now, please just accept my direction. If you are right-handed you will use your left-hand to squeeze the paper. If you are left-handed you will use your right hand.

I want you to understand that your ability and willingness to release whatever emotions come up for you is in direct proportion to the feelings and emotions themselves. When I ask you if you are able to or willing to release a particular feeling or emotion, it is perfectly acceptable for you to say, "No!" If you find yourself unwilling to release a particular feeling, I simply want you to look at what perceived benefits you feel you are getting by hanging on to it. Remember that you have "it," it does not have you! To be free of the effects of "it" **you** must be willing to release "it."

Because I cannot see you, and you cannot see the other students or me in a class, you will have to really work hard at using your creative imagination. I need to rely on you to revisit the feelings, emotions, and BELIEFS that you were unwilling to release and work on them until you have released them. This will most likely not happen at the beginning of this lesson because, as in the past, I will start you slow and easy and use simple issues that most people are willing to let go of. However, the really **big** "Wows" come to your awareness only when you are willing, truly willing to release the really **big** issues.

Please do not judge the effectiveness of this process until you have used it on some **big**, important, and powerful issues. When you do, you will experience a **big** benefit!

If you'll think back to a time when you experienced a serious emotional upset, you will see that you have used a similar process to release those emotional feelings and experiences. Your method might have been blowing your top or crying out your feelings to the point of release and relief.

You will be pleased to learn that this form of the BRT will give you a simpler, more socially acceptable way of ridding yourself of those same intense feelings, before they overwhelm you and the people around you.

Before we begin, as with all of the **success systems** you will learn from me, it is critically important that you not be interrupted for the next 30 minutes. If you have not taken the time and the steps to be sure of your complete and total privacy, please do so now.

Take a deep cleansing breath and allow yourself to relax. Take your **control** piece of paper into your non-dominant hand and hold it gently. Let's begin with something simple and easy. Recall a time when you were driving your car and someone else did something to you that caused you to feel angry or scared. Slowly, gradually, recall the event. Slowly, gradually, allow the event to take form in your mind and start to re-experience the emotions you felt. Put yourself back in the situation. Recall all of the details of where you were going, what you were doing, what you were thinking as this event occurred. Recall it all, in as much detail as possible. Now, remember the event just as it happened. Be willing to feel all of the emotions as you experienced them at that time. Are you feeling them? Good!

Notice that as you experience this event again that you are also re-experiencing the same emotions that you experienced during the actual event. Allow yourself to reexperience all of the feelings. What emotions are you feeling right now? Do you see that the feelings and emotions from this event are still with you? Your ability and willingness to reexperience this moment in the past, to a great extent controls your ability to release it. If you can still feel the feelings and emotions from this event, you not only can, but also must release them. This part of the exercise should have already demonstrated to you that on an emotional and BELIEF level, your past is still very much a part of your present.

Allow yourself to completely reexperience this past moment and memory. Let yourself feel and reexperience all of your emotions about this event. Wouldn't it be wonderful if you could release these BELIEFS, emotions, feelings, and associated memories forever? Here is yet another Steven Lloyd-ism.

> *"Understand that YOU have these BELIEFS, emotions, feelings, and associated memories-they do NOT have you!"*

So it is possible for you to release them if you are willing to do so.

Let me ask you this question: Is it possible, just possible, for you to be willing to release these **control** BELIEFS, emotions, feelings, and associated memories? If you said, "Yes," squeeze your control paper as if you are grabbing onto these BELIEFS, emotions, feelings, and associated memories. Do you understand and perceive the benefit of releasing these **control** BELIEFS, emotions, feelings, and associated memories? If you said "Yes", squeeze harder!

Now, let me ask this question: Are you willing to release the BELIEFS, emotions, feelings, and associated memories of this event? If you answered, "Yes," squeeze tighter as if you are grabbing onto and holding the control BELIEFS, emotions, feelings, and associated memories of this event. Squeeze them really hard! Now, answer this question: When are you willing to release all of the **control** BELIEFS, emotions, feelings and associated memories of this event? If you answered, "Now," take a deep breath, release your fist and your paper. Blow as hard as you can on your open hand. As you blow all of the air in your lungs onto your open hand, see the **control** paper fly from your hand taking with it all of these **control** BELIEFS, emotions, feelings, and associated memories that you have been suppressing since that moment of impact. Feel all of the BELIEFS, emotions, feelings, and associated memories leaving your mind, body, and spirit now!

When you first begin, it may take you several sessions like this one to be able to release all of the BELIEFS, emotions, feelings, and associated memories that you have linked to a negative experience. Reprocessing the exact same event over and over again until it is completely released is the only way I have discovered to teach you how to master this process. So pick up your piece of paper that says "**security**" and let's do this again.

You will probably notice that the BELIEFS, emotions, feelings, and associated memories are less dramatic than the first time you did this exercise. It is, however, very important to process ALL of the BELIEFS, emotions, feelings, and associated memories until you can only recall the event but it has no emotions or feelings left in it. So, revisit in your mind the memory of this auto incident. See yourself in your car and run your mental videotape forward all the way to the point where someone did something to you where you experienced a negative emotion. See and feel yourself in that moment once again. Allow yourself to get hold of and reexperience the feelings. As you do, put those feelings and memories of lack of **security** inside the piece of paper in your hand and squeeze it gently. Let me ask you again, is it possible for you to release your BELIEFS, emotions, feelings, and associated memories? If you said, "Yes," squeeze your paper and all of the BELIEFS, emotions, feelings, and associated memories tighter. Do you understand the benefit of releasing these BELIEFS, emotions, feelings and associated memories? If you said "Yes", squeeze harder. Is it possible for you to release these BELIEFS, emotions, feelings and associated memories completely? If you answered, "Yes," squeeze really hard! Put all of the negative energy of these BELIEFS, emotions, feelings, and associated memories into your fist! One last question, when are you willing to completely release it all? If you answered, "Now," take a deep breath and as you blow all of the BELIEFS, emotions, feelings, and associated memories out of your hand, feel the feelings and emotions leaving your mind, body, and spirit now! See and experience the BELIEFS and associated memories moving away from you, out into the atmosphere. Feel a complete sense of release and relief. Take another deep cleansing breath and slowly release the breath from your lips, blowing away any remaining control or security BELIEFS, emotions, feelings, and associated memories about this experience.

Now, revisit your automobile scenario again. Do you notice a change in the way you feel and recall this event? Please allow me to prove to you how valuable and important this process is. Repeat this process with me one more time. This time, put all four pieces of paper in your hand. Recall the event in your mind, and activate as many of the BELIEFS, emotions, feelings, and associated memories as possible from this past event.

I know this may be difficult because most of it is already gone, but repeat the same process by recalling the BELIEFS, emotions, feelings, and associated memories to mind. Put the remaining BELIEFS, emotions, feelings, and associated memories into your pieces of paper and squeeze gently. Now, let me ask you if it is possible for you to completely release the remaining BELIEFS, emotions, feelings, and associated memories of this event? If you said, "Yes," squeeze your pieces of paper harder. Are you willing to release all of the BELIEFS, emotions, feelings, and associated memories of this event? If you said, "Yes," squeeze harder! Do you understand the benefit of remaining BELIEFS, emotions, feelings, and associated memories? If you said, "Yes," squeeze harder! When are you willing to let them all go completely? If you answered, "Now," take a deep breath, and blow all of the BELIEFS, emotions, feelings, and associated memories out of your hand along with the pieces of paper, and feel them leave your mind, body, and spirit!

How do you feel? Try to recall the event. Do you notice a change? Try to find the original BELIEFS, emotions, feelings, and associated memories of the experience. Do you notice a change? Most people answer, "Yes!" If you still have any significant charge from this event, continue to repeat this process until it is completely gone.

If you feel somewhat uncomfortable with this process, relax and just go with it. It is completely normal and understandable for you not to be comfortable with something that you are new at. One of the *golden keys* that unlocks your door to success is your willingness to be uncomfortable with something that you are new at. Be willing to be new until you become good at it. Follow the same formula past good to excellent and on to World-Class! It is the same process every World-Class salesperson has followed to get where they are.

Here's something interesting: Pick up your four pieces of paper and let's do this same exercise one more time! Notice how your brain is saying, "No, no, no, it's gone!" I do not want or need to even think about that event again!" Don't you find that amazing? Just a few hundred words ago you wanted to strangle the guy who cut you off in traffic!

Just a few hundred words ago you could recall the feelings and emotions to the point of feeling stress in your body and now you can hardly recall the event at all! Why is that? The BRT **success system**! Keep using this system for processing negative events, and you will be amazed and delighted with the increase of your personal power and abilities!

It is my opinion that this BRT process CAUSES an electronic change in the path codes to our BELIEFS. When this occurs, our emotions and associated memories change. It is not that we cannot recall them, they simply do not have the same value! I am sure you know that your brain sends out electronic energy. It can be measured on several electronic devices, some of which measures your brain waves. When you die, the brain stops sending waves. Most of these brain wave activities are involuntary. Think of your brain waves as beams of light pouring out of your mind like waves of electricity. The vast majority, millions if not billions per day, fire off from one hemisphere of your brain to the other. Every now and then, something happens to "ground" that thought or experience into a sub-field of consciousness (a BELIEF) within your consciousness (your mind). The intensity of the energy generated from this event (emotion), which grounds your thoughts or your experience, determines the size and intensity of your new BELIEF (program).

Let me give you an example. Ask yourself about the BELIEF we just released. How many times do you drive from point A to point B, event free? "Most of the time," is the typical answer that I get from my students. So, in other words, your brain is sailing along feeling just fine with all of its little actions, reactions, issues, and events that show up on a typical day of driving. 99% of the time, you are in brain heaven, right?

Well, examine the following three examples. One day someone drives just a little too close to you and their move requires you to put on your brakes to keep from getting hit. Not a major event, but enough of an interruption for you to store the event in your Stupid Driver memory file. As you pass the other driver and look over at them with that Stupid Idiot look of yours, you see an embarrassed face and read the words, "I'm sorry," on their lips. What happens? Your brain pulls this little event out of your I'm Angry For The Rest Of My Life file and releases it.

Follow along with me through the next scenario. Play the exact same driving scenario as above except, this time, you pull up next to this driver and he gives you one-half of a peace sign! You know, the hand signal that indicates his IQ. What happens in your brain now? Do you recall this event and play it over and over and over again until everyone who knows you does not want to listen to it anymore? Sure you do, we all do!

The last scene is exactly the same as the above two scenes with one change in the outcome of this scene. As you pull up next to the other driver to give him one of your famous Stupid Idiot looks, this driver slams into your car and forces you off the road. As both cars come to a stop, he gets out of his car, pulls a baseball bat out from the backseat, and starts running towards your car with an enraged look on his face. Is there any doubt in your mind that at that very moment you are building a BELIEF that you will carry for the rest of your life, if it is not released? Each person will associate this experience differently and with different value and power, but this is exactly how it works!

There are some people who would associate such lack of **control** and or lack of **security**, that they may never drive again! Remember, in a moment of intensity the normal thought process is interrupted and a BELIEF is formed. What that belief is labeled is what determines how you react from that moment forward.

You probably have equally intense stored BELIEFS that must be released for you to experience and express your true potential. There is not just one way to release and replace these and other forms of limiting BELIEFS; however, congratulations on finding one new way to achieving just that, here and now! This **success system** and technology will work for you if you will work with it.

BELIEF Replacement Training will give you a new way of looking at why and how you personally react to, or respond to situations the way you do. BRT will also set the stage for you to start understanding how and why your prospective clients respond to you the way they do. BRT will also give you the tools to change these BELIEFS into a positive **success system** of human interaction that will serve you and your clients for years to come.

Another awareness I have observed and learned from in my years of research of how the brain receives and retrieves input, data, and emotions, leads us to the next lesson called, **Brain Language**.

Before we move on to that subject, I encourage you to use the BRT techniques I have outlined for you and to keep processing, releasing, and replacing your negative BELIEFS. This process is much like peeling an onion. Just when you think you have finished, another layer shows up. If you will stay the course, you will process all of your stuff, all the way down to the most powerful, most productive part of you, your

Heart! If you will do this work, I promise someday very soon you will meet one of the greatest people to ever live. You will meet the real **you**!

Now, let's move on to learn how your brain and the brains you come in contact with everyday think, process information, and what brain language they speak. Keep reading. The next chapter will absolutely revolutionize the way you communicate and sell!

CHAPTER ELEVEN
BRAIN LANGUAGE

LEARNING TO SPEAK THEIR LANGUAGE

After you master this chapter, you will take your life and career to a level of productivity, prosperity, and functionality that you only dreamed was possible. This chapter will also prepare you for World-Class sales closing unlike anything you have ever seen before.

Imagine what it will do for your personal, professional, and financial lives when you always know, understand, and communicate with the brain language and dialect someone else is speaking. Picture how quickly you will be able to build rapport with someone when they truly understand your visual, auditory, kinesthetic, patriarchal and matriarchal input, ideas, concepts, and solutions based on which language and dialect that they speak.

Think back to a sale that you made where you and the person you were selling to, just clicked. As you recall this event, notice how both the language you and they spoke matched, as well as the way or style in which you communicated paired together to make a bond between you. Remember how fast this happened? Do you recall how easy, simple, fast, and fun it was to make this sale? What if you could repeat this same scenario by adopting a **success system** that worked the same way with almost everyone you met? Sound too good to be true? Well, that picture is not only possible, it is already happening!

Think back to a time when you were presenting to more than one person at a time when, for some reason, you didn't seem to click with one or more of the prospects. Why did this happen? What is it that CAUSES rapport to happen with some people and not others?

If you examine each scenario closely, you will find that one of two things is happening. First, you and your prospect spoke the same brain language and the same dialect. If both of your brain languages were auditory, you and they most likely found it difficult to stop talking. If both of you spoke with a patriarchal dialect, you probably talked and talked about all kinds of issues from business and politics to sports. If both of you spoke with a matriarchal dialect, you most likely talked and talked about issues and experiences like family, friends, team efforts, and relationships.

In the not-so-successful sales memory, you were connected with and communicated very well with one person, but not the other. When a person is not spoken to in his or her language and dialect, he or she feels overlooked, neglected, ignored, unappreciated, or disliked. Lack of rapport and lack of their support and personal interest in your sale is the result.

Regardless of how you recall your past two sales scenarios, just notice that you seem to be able to communicate with a specific type of brain language and dialect combination better than others. What will your income look like when you are able to have the same successful relationship results as you did in your successful sales scenario with almost everyone you meet? PDR the lessons in this chapter and you will be able to immediately use all six of the brain language and dialect combinations. Six may sound like a lot but remember, you already speak one of the brain language and dialect combinations fluently, so you only need to study, learn, and PDR the other five. After working with the lessons that I am giving you in this chapter, students of mine have increased their sales performance 25% to 1000%, and you will too!

This chapter is called brain language for a very good reason. Each of us receives, processes, stores, retrieves, communicates, and responds in one of three brain languages. These languages are visual, auditory, and kinesthetic. We also speak one of two dialects. These dialects are patriarchal and matriarchal. Think of someone you know that speaks Spanish. What type of Spanish do they speak: Mexican, Puerto Rican, South American, Cuban or Spanish from Spain?

You may have heard of the two developers of NLP, Richard Bandler and John Grinder. These men built on the pioneer mind science work done by Dr. Milton Erickson. Their years of research prove that each of us thinks in one of three modalities (brain languages). I call them brain languages because you will have an easier time understanding and therefore using this information if your brain doesn't get hung up wondering what the word modality means. The term brain language is a more functional term and actually describes how this brain process works.

Again, there are three basic languages. They are visual, auditory, and kinesthetic. We all possess all three of these qualities and can speak all three of these languages as needed or prompted. As you study the qualities and characteristics of these different brain languages, don't debate with yourself which one you are. You may notice that you have a lot of another quality as well as your dominant language. What is normally the case is that your second language is very close to your dominant language. Also, please do not fall victim to BELIEVING that one brain language is better than another. They are what they are, and you are who you are. Each of us has our own special qualities, gifts, talents, and abilities. Often, when you have two brain languages that are very close to each other, you are what I call bilingual. It is sometimes difficult to determine which is your dominant language. In a few people, all three of the brain languages are either equal in dominance or so close together that no dominant language can be determined. These people are able to move easily from one brain language to another and are called fully integrated or tri-lingual.

Again, the two different dialects are patriarchal and matriarchal. Later I will give you lists of words that will help you understand and be able to identify these two dialects better. I will also show you how to redesign your presentations to present and communicate to each of your prospects in their specific brain language and dialect. Greater and faster rapport will be the result because you will speak their language. As you master this technology, you will see another **success system** that you will have so much fun working with! It is almost like having the entire world open up to you by being able to speak all of the major languages and dialects.

I have provided you with tests in this chapter so you can determine your dominant brain language as well as your own dialect. I will also teach you how to determine what language and dialect other people are speaking. More importantly, you will learn how to speak their language and dialect too.

You will see the benefit of speaking both the language and the dialect of the person you are wanting to connect with the very first time you use it. You will experience for yourself that using this **success system** will allow you to reach people like nothing you have ever tried before. It is as powerful as fluently speaking both the language and dialect of someone from a foreign country. They not only like you more for speaking their language, they love you for trying. Rapport and that magical "click" happen almost instantly! Using this brain language and dialect **success system** is the fastest way to get people to like, BELIEVE, and trust you. The great news is that you don't have to master this chapter to start using this **success system** and start receiving the benefits. You will start receiving the benefits during the PDR section of this chapter.

The following explanations are for those brains that process right-handed. If you or your prospect is left-handed, the eye-movement will be reversed. The exceptions are rare and normally apply to those people who are ambidextrous (use both hands with equal ease). Normally, even with those who are ambidextrous, the movements are consistently one direction or the other, regardless of which hand they use to write with. I'm not going to invest any time here discussing these specific variations because they are very rare. Study these following explanations and examples. I will discuss fully integrated, trilingual people and co-dialectal thinkers later because you may meet, or perhaps are, one of these types of thinkers. The eye chart that I have provided you will be helpful to your understanding of this process. As I explain each brain language, you can look at the eye chart to see the eye movements of each brain language.

Brain Language Eye Movement Chart

Visual Constructed

Auditory Constructed

Kinesthetic Constructed

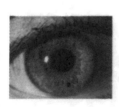
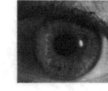
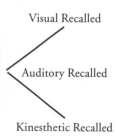

Visual Recalled

Auditory Recalled

Kinesthetic Recalled

Right Hand Example

THE VISUAL THINKER

Let's start with the visual brain language. Right-handed Visual thinkers will move their eyes up and to the left to recall and up and to the right to think or construct thought. The procedure to test for any brain language is to ask recall type questions like, "I'm just curious, what was the name of the very first sales manager you had, do you recall?" Or, you might ask, "What was the name of your high school principal, do you recall?" You will see their eyes go to work searching their brain for any answer that is not in what I call the Resident Access Memory or RAM. An example of a RAM type of question that does not cause a brain language response eye movement is; "What is the name of your oldest child, do you recall?" He or she does not need to retrieve that information because they know it and most probably use the information on a regular basis.

Again, Visual thinkers will move their eyes up and to the left to recall and up and to the right when they are thinking or constructing thought. They also may look straight ahead as if they are daydreaming or looking straight through you when they are thinking. Their eyes will refocus when they have finished thinking. If you are in a selling situation, never interrupt a Visual thinker's "stare" because they are deep in thought. If you interrupt this thought, you will lose rapport because you interrupted their constructive thought process. It is not easy for them to recapture what they were thinking about. Visual thinkers will not give you a positive buying decision unless and until you give them the time to look at all of the angles. Visual people may appear to take a long time to make up their minds. This is because they need to see everything that relates to their decision. *Selling From The Heart* students know this and plan in advance to bring all of the pictures, graphs, charts, and other visual information that a Visual may need to make an informed decision on the first sales call. Visual people are easy to sell, however you must have all of the possibilities covered to their satisfaction before they will say "Yes."

You can identify Visual thinkers by the Visual words that dominate their dialogue.

VISUAL WORDS

APPEAR	IMAGINATION	SEEN
APPEARANCE	INSPECT	SHOW
EXAMINE	INVESTIGATE	SHOWN
EXHIBIT	LOOK	SPECTACLE
EXHIBITION	LOOKED	SPY
EXPOSE	NOTICE	STARE
EYE	OBSERVE	VIEW
GAZE	PICTURE	VISUAL
GLANCE	PICTORIAL	VISUALIZE
GLIMPSE	SAW	WATCH
IMAGINE	SEE	WITNESS

You can also identify Visual thinkers by the visual phrases that they use.

VISUAL PHRASES

"**Show** me...."

"I would like to **see**..."

"What does the **picture look** like to you?"

"I **see** it more like this..."

"What's wrong with this **picture**?"

"From my point of **view**..."

"How do you **see** it?"

You need three indicators or successful tests to determine someone's brain language. To be sure you are working with a Visual thinker, you should have **both** the successful visual brain language eye movement test, as well as the visual words and or phrases dominating their dialogue test.

Visual thinkers tend to rise to the highest levels of leadership in business, industry, education, and government because they really do see the "big picture." A Visual thinker's brain can process information so fast that, if they are not careful, they can overwhelm the other two types of brain language thinkers. Their brain speed is so fast because they think in pictures.

Within each picture is a thousand words or experiences. They have the ability and tendency to download or ask for uploads of massive amounts of information that can be so intense for an Auditory or a Kinesthetic that it can cause "smoke" to roll out of their ears trying to process the information at a Visual's speed. When pressed for a decision that a Visual thinker is not prepared to make, a Visual will often say, "Let me look it over and I will get back to you."

Selling From The Heart students always use brain language tests or trial closes based on the brain language they are presenting to. If you know that your prospect is a Visual thinker, you may use a test or trial close like, "How does this **look** to you so far?" If you have done a good job of visual presentation, your Visual prospects will normally respond with something like, "It looks good so far, what else do you have to show me?" After your first test question or trial close with Visual thinkers, do not proceed until they have agreed that it **looks** good or acceptable to your current point of presentation. If you do proceed without the positive response, Visual thinkers will almost always end the interview with, "Let me **look** it over again and we will get back to you!" What they are really saying is, "You have not **shown** me the information, data, or details in a format and at a speed to hold my attention to the point of decision." Remember that they cannot **see** what you are saying!

Again, Visual thinkers can process more information in a shorter time than the other two brain language thinkers can. These are the prospects that normally say, "**Show** me the bottom line!" Why? Because you are boring them! Most pre-designed sales presentations do not consider the different brain languages that will be experiencing the presentation. They are normally written and designed by an Auditory salesperson or sales manager. These general presentations are normally most effective with Auditories. The presentations that include visual aids with pictures, graphs, and color images **combined** with visual words almost always appeal to two thirds of the market. Those presentations that additionally include the touch, feel, and emotional aspects of the product or service, appeal to and enroll the missing Kinesthetic third to complete 100% of your market and your sales results.

To determine how your presentation is structured, simply read a transcribed version of the actual audiocassette taped presentation. Note the times you hear Auditory words like: **sound, hear, heard, listened, speak,**

spoken, talk, etc. Repeat this same process for each of the other two brain languages. You will be amazed at what you discover. This is one of the CAUSES of the average sales closing ratio being around 33%. What would your closing ratio be if two-thirds of your prospects spoke two other languages other than English and you did not speak their languages?

Heart Selling presentations are designed to consider all three of the brain languages, coupled with the Patriarchal and Matriarchal dialects for a total of six brain language and dialect combinations.

The first step to successfully redesigning your sales presentation is, awareness. Simply being aware that two-thirds of your sales audience speaks a different brain language than you do is a great start. Auditory presentations are too slow and too wordy for Visual thinkers and are too fast and lack the elements that allow the Kinesthetic thinkers to experience the presentation in a physical or emotional way. You can and will significantly increase your sales effectiveness by adjusting your speed, information flow, and communication language to the speed, information flow, and communication language of your prospect.

THE AUDITORY THINKER

Next is the Auditory brain language. Again, allow me to remind you that the examples I am using are for right-handed auditory thinkers. If you are a good communicator, you are most likely an Auditory. When asked recall questions, an auditory thinker's eyes will move laterally left toward the left ear to recall and laterally right towards the right ear to think or construct thought.

You can identify Auditory thinkers by the words that dominate their dialogue.

AUDITORY WORDS

ADDRESS	CONFESS	DIVULGE
ANNOUNCE	DECLARE	EXPLAIN
ARTICULATE	DESCRIBE	EXPRESS
ARTICULATION	DIALECT	HEAR
CHATTER	DICTION	HEARD
COMMUNICATE	DISCUSS	HUSHED

INFORM	MENTION	QUIET
INSTRUCT	MUTE	RECANT
JARGON	NARRATE	RECITE
LANGUAGE	NOISY	SAID
LECTURE	OVERHEAR	SAY
LINGO	PREACH	SAYS
LISTEN	PRONOUNCE	SCOLD
LISTENED	PRONUNCIATION	SERMON

You can also identify auditory thinkers by the Auditory phrases that they use.

"**Hear** me!"

"I would like to **hear**…"

"What does it **sound** like to you?"

"I **hear** you!"

"What did he or she **say**?"

"I **hear** that!"

"**Because** I **said** so."

When nervous, uncomfortable, or angry, Auditory thinkers will almost always talk too much. This is one of the main reasons many sales companies have required scripted presentations that their salespeople must learn and use. Auditories will think out loud, trying to talk their way back to the point they were trying to make or remember. I am sure you have heard the old phrase, "He talked his way past the sale."

The skill, ability, and talent to speak well is an Auditory thinker's greatest asset, but also their biggest weakness. If you are an Auditory, you have experienced a time when you wish you had kept your mouth shut!

Why do Auditories talk so much? They are trying to get people to communicate with them! Somewhere, within most Auditory brain language thinkers, there is a BELIEF that says, "Talking equals approval," or "Talking means the other person likes me." If you are an Auditory brain language thinker, does this sound familiar? Would you say that what I have said is correct? Does that sound like it makes sense to you? How does that sound to you? Agree? Yes? Correct? Auditory thinkers crave feedback and acknowledgement as much as Visual thinkers need to **see** results or Kinesthetic thinkers need to **feel** comfortable. Auditories are, however, the ones with their self-esteem on the line, offering all or most of the information, leaving themselves open and vulnerable. Auditory thinkers also feel better when they are talking. Most Auditories love to talk. They will talk to almost anyone. They even talk to themselves when no one else is around. You can always tell the Auditory drivers at the red light. They are the ones carrying on conversations with themselves!

I, too, struggled with the downside of being an Auditory. One of the secrets I discovered through exhaustive research and observation was that you could be a great conversationalist by just listening! I noticed that the people that I enjoyed being around had all mastered the art and science of active listening.

Remember that two of our greatest human **needs,** regardless of our brain languages, are **approval** and **acceptance.** If your goal is to gain approval and acceptance, how better to get people to like you then to listen to them? Think back to when you met some special people, at a party or other social gathering, that everyone seemed to like and enjoy. Notice that they all seemed to have one special quality: they all listened! They may have been good storytellers or speakers but they were also **active listeners.** They asked open-ended questions that began with who, what, where, when, why, and how. They got you talking and kept you talking. We Auditory thinkers need to understand that our greatest skills and abilities as communicators can be multiplied and magnified by listening. Communication in all of its forms, including selling, is a team sport and no one likes a ball hog!

I use and teach a communications game that helps to build your listening skills and abilities. Most people like to play games. The game is called mental tennis. Here are the rules. You must answer every question with a question. You can make a statement as long as it ends with a question. The game is scored the same way tennis is scored, love (zero), 15, 30, 40, and game. It is a great exercise for all three of the brain languages. For Auditory thinkers, it teaches us to lob the ball back to someone else in the conversation. For both the Visual and Kinesthetic thinkers it helps to develop stronger communication skills by requiring them to keep the conversation going. It is a great mental exercise because it requires ending each statement with a question, giving the other person an opportunity to respond. Try it, you will love it!

THE KINESTHETIC THINKER

Kinesthetic brain language thinkers are the most misunderstood of all of the brain language thinkers. A Kinesthetic tends to be a person of few words. Kinesthetics are often referred to as aloof, stuck up, or shy. This BELIEF was born because of the ways Kinesthetics process information. Their eyes move down and to the left to recall information and down and to the right to think or construct thought. They often lower their head as well as their eyes during the contemplative thought process. Kinesthetic thinkers tend to avoid confrontation; they are often mistaken for being passive or even submissive. Kinesthetic thinkers are also BELIEVED to be emotional. Although it is true that Kinesthetic thinkers process information and think through their emotions, they are not necessarily emotional. Casual and uninformed observers often make serious mistakes in trying to work with and understand the Kinesthetic thinker.

In addition to the unique lower eye movements, you can identify the Kinesthetic thinkers by the words that dominate their dialogue.

KINESTHETIC WORDS

ACCOMPANY	FELT	SENSE
ACHIEVE	FOLLOW	SENSATION
ADOPT	FOUND	SENSIBILITY
AFFECTION	GUIDED	SENSITIVITY
ATTEND	LEAD	SENTIMENT
ATTITUDE	MAKE	SPONTANEOUS
AVOID	MANNER	SYMPATHY
BE	MOOD	TAKE
BEING	MANNERISM	TENDERNESS
BEARING	PASSION	TRACK
CARRY ON	PEACEFUL	TRAIL
CHASE	PERPETRATE	UNDERSTAND
COMPASSION	PRODUCE	UNDERSTANDING
DO	PROPENSITY	VISIT
DOING	PURSUE	WITH
EMOTION	PUT	WORK
FEEL	RESULT	

You can also identify Kinesthetic thinkers by the kinesthetic phrases that they use.

"I **understand** how you **feel**!"

"I would like you to **understand**…"

"What does it **feel** like to you?"

"I am **with** you!"

"What did he or she **experience**?"

"I **follow** you!"

"**Meet with** them and…"

Because Kinesthetic thinkers tend to use emotional terms, many people inaccurately assume that they are always emotional or subject to their emotions. Kinesthetic thinkers do distance themselves from their emotions. You may witness them sitting, looking at you with a stone cold look on their face. Once Kinesthetic thinkers realize that their emotions are the CAUSE of their pain or the cause of their being manipulated, they will often put a wall between you and them, making it difficult to reach them emotionally.

Kinesthetic thinkers take the longest amount of time of the three brain language thinkers to process information because the avenue of reception to the area of retention in their brain is the longest path of all of the three brain languages. However, once the Kinesthetic thinkers "get it," they almost never forget it!

Kinesthetic thinkers need to experience what they are learning to truly grasp and understand the information. Until and unless you truly understand the Kinesthetic thinker you will become frustrated trying to teach, coach, or sell to them. However, if you will study what I am teaching you here, and learn how to communicate with Kinesthetic thinkers, you will find them some of the most loyal and committed friends, associates, or clients you will ever have.

If you are in a personal or business relationship with a Kinesthetic thinker, it is important that you understand what kinds of attention they respond to. They respond best to gentle, sincere demonstrations of attention. They are normally non-assertive and prosper best in non-confrontational environments that require the least amount of the use of their communication skills.

Kinesthetic thinkers prefer to write rather than use the phone. You will normally find Kinesthetic thinkers in support roles requiring the least amount of social interaction, or at the top surrounded by people who guard them and take care of the communications needs for them. Many Kinesthetic thinkers are misunderstood from birth, through education and on into employment as well as in marriage.

Kinesthetic students can and often are referred to as "slow" or even told that there is something wrong with them. These cruel, inaccurate, and ignorant messages almost always come from Auditory or Visual teachers who are trying to get their students to learn in the same ways they did. The vast majority of teachers teach every student by means of their own brain language, leaving the Kinesthetic thinkers to struggle on their own to receive, retain, and test based on the teacher's language of delivering the information.

Dr. Albert Einstein, one of the greatest thinkers of all time and recently voted the most significant person to live in the last 1000 years, was a Kinesthetic thinker. Throughout his early years in school he was told that he was slow and even retarded. He was kicked out of his eighth-grade math class for being a dunce. Well, the teacher was 50% right, one of them was a dunce, but it was **not** Einstein!

It is human nature that we are uncomfortable with people that are unlike us and that we tend to reward, enjoy, and associate with people that appear to be the most like us. Think back to your own grade school education. The teacher's pet was almost always an Auditory or a Visual thinker, just like the teacher. The next time you see a group of people that hang out together, study them closely. You will notice that they are like clones of each other. This is the CAUSE of adolescents dyeing their hair or piercing their noses or wearing their pants so that their underwear shows. They are all trying to look alike and be accepted by all of the kids in that same peer group, while at the same time claiming that they are doing it in the name of individuality. You and I both know that they are conforming and not expressing their uniqueness. We can take a lesson from this and apply it in the business of sales. This time look at a group of teenagers that flock together like ducks all heading the wrong way. Step out of your judgement and ask yourself what the CAUSE is. Notice how they all stand and move the same way. Hear their words and voice tonality and notice how they all look, walk, dress, and sound the same.

What happens when other kids walk by this group and happen to be wearing something different? They tease and ridicule them and make fun of them for not looking, sounding, and acting just as they do! Yet, don't we do exactly the same thing in our own way? If you joined a company that had casual day on Friday and the peer group you were part of wore blue jeans on Friday, how long would it take you to start wearing blue jeans on Fridays? If you were invited to an inner sales circle where only the big hitters get to go, what is one of the first things you would want to know? The kind of clothes everyone else will be wearing, right? Why? This happens because we all have human NEEDS for **approval** and **acceptance**.

Although peer pressure is intense for all three of the brain language thinkers, social interaction is the most difficult for the Kinesthetic thinkers because they are the least expressive of the three brain language thinkers. When you see them at a social function you may think that they are bored or shy because they are normally not interacting with other people. Yet, what is really happening is that they are experiencing the entire party. They don't miss anything unless and until they are engaged in conversation with a particular person who has their total attention. Then they see, hear, and experience nothing else.

Unless Kinesthetic thinkers have a well-defined secondary auditory brain language, they should be encouraged to develop one before entering professional sales or any of the communication business disciplines. This is for the same reason you would not encourage an Auditory thinker to enter the accounting field until and unless he or she develops his or her kinesthetic or visual brain language. Additionally, Auditory thinkers need to learn how to shut off their auditory mechanism during non-auditory events.

With the proper training, Kinesthetic thinkers can perform well in auditory or visual disciplines. However, they will excel naturally in the areas that are more suited for their kinesthetic nature. Normally, if Kinesthetic thinkers are selected for auditory positions like receptionists, they will fail unless they have trained their auditory abilities. If Kinesthetic thinkers express themselves in a voice and volume that is natural for them, people will be shouting at them saying, "Speak up, we can't hear you!" Conversely, if you put Auditory thinkers into the accounting department without training them on how to control their auditory qualities, no one gets any bookkeeping done, because the Auditory thinkers are talking to everyone! When you match people's dominant brain language to specific job functions, magic happens!

This explains why top salespeople who are promoted into management almost always struggle and often fail. The brain language and skills used to succeed in sales are completely different than those required for succeeding in management. Remember that you can learn to speak and function very well in other brain languages, but you must first recognize that they exist. Next, you must understand which brain language is required for success in a particular discipline. Most importantly, you must discipline your brain to use only that language until success is achieved. Remember, we all have all three of the brain language abilities within us and available to us, but we must develop them.

Selling is both an art form and a science. The best, most effective salespeople have mastered both the art of the presentation by having good people skills, as well as the science side or the business of selling. The science side of selling is the discipline of running a sales business. That discipline or skill set is the required prospecting, appointment setting, record-keeping and ongoing client follow-up. The salespeople whose production is up one month and down the next are trying to achieve and maintain World-Class sales performance just by using only the art form of the presentation and people skills. This is only one of the two skill sets required to run, grow, and maintain a successful sales business. This would be like climbing into a boxing ring with one arm tied behind your back and being surprised when you lose the fight!

The bridge from one skill set to another is the activation of the brain language that corresponds to the needed skill or discipline. Top sales performers normally use their auditory skills as their dominant brain language. Good and effective business people or managers on the other hand, need their visual skills to analyze reports, charts, budgets, and to write correspondence. They use their kinesthetic qualities and abilities to feel the personality traits of support staff in order to maintain ongoing business relationships. By working with the brain language information this book provides you and developing all three of your brain languages and then applying them to both of the required sides of your sales business, you will achieve and maintain World-Class sales performance.

Well, what can one brain language person do to catch up fast with the qualities and benefits of another brain language? I have developed a **success system** to increase your brain language perceptions and abilities dramatically, in just one day. First, you need to determine which brain language is most dominant for you.

Here is an effective test. First, write out a two-page story in a narrative format. The two pages should be on 8½ x 11 size paper. Write a narrative report on where you grew up and went to grade school. Write about your hometown, where you went to school, who you played with and some of the things you did. Add as much detail as you possibly can. Provide as much recall information as possible. **Please stop reading now and do this exercise.** If you continue to read the following information before you do this exercise, it will negatively affect your test results and thereby render them worthless. **Please stop reading now and do this exercise.**

Now that you have completed your exercise, take a red pen and circle all of the visual words like: "**see, saw, view, looked, seen, picture,**" etc. When you have finished circling the visual words, count them. Now record your count on a separate sheet of paper.

Next take a different color pen say, blue or green, and circle all of the auditory words like: "**hear, heard, listened, speak, spoken, said, says,**" etc. Repeat the counting and recording process.

Lastly, take a third color pen and circle all of the kinesthetic words like: "**feel, felt, found, follow, being, doing,**" etc. Now, record the number of kinesthetic words.

Once you have completed the above exercise and counted the number of auditory, visual and kinesthetic words, you are ready to chart your results. Create a simple chart showing which brain language is the most dominant. Next, list the brain language that is the second most dominant. Finally, list the brain language that is the least dominant. Notice the distance between the numbers on your chart. Determine the percentile ratio between your first brain language and your second brain language. Then determine the percentile ratio between your first and third brain language. This will show you how close your first language is to your second and your third.

Next, you need to determine which brain language you need to develop, improve, and strengthen. Let's say you are Kinesthetic thinker and you just accepted a job as a salesperson. Your auditory brain language skills and abilities need to be developed, improved, and be enhanced immediately! Use the following technique and you will be amazed and delighted how quickly your auditory skills and abilities will develop, improve, and strengthen in just one day!

Your first step is to sit down with a notepad and write out every auditory (or whatever brain language you are working on) word you can think of. Now, take two new sheets of paper and rewrite the same story you wrote earlier. This time, however, I want you to rewrite the story in the brain language that you are developing. This will be a stretch for you, but BELIEVE me, it is the fastest way to activate your desired brain language and communication process. The desired result for this lesson is to get you to think in a new brain language.

Your next task is to think, speak, and write in that brain language for the rest of the day. If you will do this exercise, you will be amazed and delighted at your improvement in such a short time. Imagine what you can achieve in one week! Most of us respond better to learning if we make learning fun. So, let's make this a game. Keep a 3x5 card with you as a scorecard. Start with 100 points. For each time you slip back to your dominant brain language, deduct one point. If you finish the day with a score of 75 or higher, you win!

INCREASING YOUR SALES AND YOUR CLOSING RATIOS

I promised you that I would show you how to increase your sales and close ratio by 25% to 1000%. This will require a lot of work on your part, but the reward per hour invested will prove to be phenomenal!

What if I took you to a country where everyone there spoke one of three languages and only one of those languages was English and that was the only language you spoke. What would you do to make a living as a salesperson? Considering the entire population, what would your closing ratio be? If you sold everyone that spoke your language, it would be very close to what it is today. On average, the closing ratio nationwide for all salespeople is about 33%. If you found yourself in a country where only one third of the people spoke your language you would have about the same closing ratio you have now because you could only present what you sell to those people who spoke your language.

A Visual brain language thinker cannot see what an Auditory is saying. A Kinesthetic thinker cannot feel what a Visual sees. An Auditory thinker cannot hear what a Kinesthetic is feeling. The first step to dramatically increasing your sales is the awareness of the fact that two brain languages other than your own surround you. Your next step in maximizing your benefits from this **success system** is to apply what you have learned. Here is another Steven Lloyd-ism.

> *"To have a skill or ability and not use it, is just like not having the skill or ability at all."*

The quickest, easiest, and most effective way that I know of to become trilingual and to permanently move that decimal point on your paycheck to the right, is as follows:

- Write out each and every word of your presentation and situational sales closes. Again, you should tape record your presentation and closes and then transcribe your own words. When you write out your presentation from memory, you activate your visual cortex. You need to know exactly what you are saying in your current presentation and closes. Speaking it out and tape recording it will give you an accurate count of the dominant brain language words and phrases you use.

- Rewrite into the other two languages only the words that reflect your dominant brain language. You already have one of three presentations and sales closes. Now, you need to rewrite your presentation and sales closes into each brain language for the other two-thirds of your sales audience.

- Practice, drill, and rehearse (PDR) each of the two new presentations and sales closes using each of the two new brain languages. These two new presentations and sales closes must be as brain language active as your dominant brain language presentation and sales closes are now. It takes PDR to **automate** your new brain language presentations and sales closes.

- Locate two people who represent the two brain languages you are in the process of developing, improving, and strengthening. Be sure to test the person to verify that his or her brain speaks the correct language you need for this exercise. Do not tell these people what you are doing or it will make them aware of how they process information and that awareness will negatively affect your results. Then present your translated presentation and closes to each person in his or her language. Once you have completed this process, ask how he or she "felt," or, how it "looked," or, "sounded." You will be amazed and delighted at the positive feedback you will receive from each of your sample prospects.

• Now I want you to become proficient in multiple language presentations and closes. Most salespeople will present to more than one person at a time. Your presentations may include two people in a home or it may require presenting to two, three, or more people in a business setting. Understand that these additional people are invited to participate in your presentation because the decision-maker values their input. Start with two different brain languages, presenting the same material, switching back and forth between the two languages, and be sure to practice your test closes in each language. After you have done two, add in the third.

SPEAKING YOUR PROSPECT'S DIALECT

The next step in your new World-Class communication and presentation education is to determine which one of the two dialects your prospect speaks.

Again, remember the Steven Lloyd-ism.

"The clearer your understanding is, the better your results are."

The following descriptions will help you identify each of the two dialects.

Patriarchs view themselves as a single unit. They "march to the beat of a single drummer." They are sometimes referred to as lone hunters. Patriarchs BELIEVE that all decisions affect them personally. Of all of the patriarch words that you are about to review, the words that best identify Patriarchs are the words, "**I, me, mine, my, self, personally** and **private**." Patriarchs are self-focused and self-defined. The majority of their time is invested in the results, as it will affect them personally. They make great leaders because they can detach themselves from the result as it affects others. They are often too "bottom line" centered, appear to be cold and uncaring, and they are best matched with Matriarchs who have a counter-balancing brain language to add the needed Heart to the team.

Matriarchs view themselves as the unit. They are not apart from the team, they are a part of the team and the team is a part of them. Matriarchs BELIEVE that their decisions affect the entire team. Of all of the matriarch words that you are about to review, the words that best identify Matriarchs are the words, "**we, us, our, team, they, them, joint** and **collective**." Matriarchs are group focused and team defined. The majority of their time is invested in the result, as it will affect the collective or the team. They make great leaders because they have the ability and willingness to consider how their decisions will affect everyone. They have a difficult time making the decisions that will affect other members of the team negatively. They are best matched with Patriarchs who have a counter-balancing brain language and who can make the tough cuts as needed for the good of the organization.

The following pages contain words that I have categorized for you into the patriarchal and matriarchal dialects. Don't get hung up in judging them, just consider them. Also, take your written presentations and situational closes and categorize the appropriate words into the two different dialects. Create the new dialect presentations and closes combining them with the three different brain language presentations and sales closes. When you are finished you should have six different presentations and closes, one for each of the six brain language and dialect combinations that each prospect speaks. I know that this may seem like a big project, but it is easier than you think. All you really need to do is to learn to speak each of the two brain languages other than your own. Then, just be aware of the words each of the two different dialects speak. Just like with the different brain languages, it is easy because you are already comfortable with one of the two: you already speak it. Here are two lists of words that I have categorized for you to indicate the patriarchal and matriarchal dialects. Remember that these are only indicators to help you to determine which dialect you and your prospect or client are speaking.

PATRIARCHAL WORDS

ACTION	EXHIBIT	LOGICAL
AMBITION	EXPAND	MANAGE
ASSERT	FACILITATOR	MASCULINE
BOTTOM-LINE	FACT	MASTER
BRAVE	FINISH	ME
BUSINESS	FOCUS	METHOD
CALCULATE	FORCE	MINE
COERCE	FULFILL	MY
COMPLEX	GAMBLE	NEGOTIATE
CONCUR	GAIN	OBLIGATION
CONFLICT	GOAL	OUTSPOKEN
CONFRONT	GREAT	PERFORM
CONQUER	GROW	POLITICS
CONSTRUCT	HANDSOME	POWER
CONTROL	HEARTY	PRIDE
COURAGE	HEROIC	PROBLEM
CREATE	HUNT	PROTECTION
DARING	HURRY	PROVIDE
DEBATE	HUSTLE	PROUD
DECISION	I	RESCUE
DECLARATION	I'LL	RESULTS
DEMAND	I'M	SOLO
DESIGNATE	INCOME	STRENGTH
DIRECT	INCREASE	STRONG
DOMINANT	INDEPENDENT	VALIANT
EXECUTE	INDIVIDUAL	VICTORY
EXERCISE	INNOVATION	VISION
EXPEDITION	LEADER	WELL-BEING

MATRIARCHAL WORDS

ACCOMMODATE
AFFECTION
AGREEABLE
APPEASE
ASSIST
AVAILABLE
BALANCE
BLISS
BROTHERHOOD
CALM
CARE
CAREFUL
CARESS
CAUTION
CHEERFUL
CHERISH
COMMEND
COMPASSION
COMMITMENT
COMPLIANT
COMPLY
COMPROMISE
CONSIDERATE
CONSISTENT
CONSULT
DEFEND
DEFINE
DEVOTE
EMOTION
EMPATHY
ENCOURAGE
EVERYONE

FAITHFUL
FAMILY
FEAR
FEELINGS
FOLLOW
FRIEND(S)
GENTLE
GENUINE
GIVER
GUARD
GUIDE
GRACEFUL
HARMONY
HOPE
HUMANE
INSTINCTIVE
INTIMATE
INTUITIVE
KIND
LEARN
LISTEN
LOVE
LOYAL
MEASURE
MERCY
NURTURE
OPEN
ORGANIZATION
OUR
PACIFY
PARDON
PATIENCE

PEACE
POLITE
PROMISE
QUIET
RATIONAL
RECONCILE
RELATE
RELATION(S)
RELATIONSHIP(S)
REQUEST
RESPECT
RESPONSIBLE
SACRIFICE
SENSITIVE
STUDENT
SUPPORT
SYMPATHETIC
SYMPATHY
TEAM
THANKFUL
THOUGHTFUL
TOLERANT
TRANQUIL
TRUST
UNDERSTANDING
UNCONDITIONAL
UNITY
US
WE
WELL-BEING

Socrates said, "Know thyself, the life not examined is not worth living." This process will help you recognize which dialect your brain speaks. Just like the brain language itself, the dialect is important. Learning to speak the other dialect will dramatically improve your rapport building skills, which will automatically increase your sales, which will in turn increase your income, which will increase your feelings of self-worth, which will increase your self-esteem! If you will invest the time needed for you to master this chapter, you will be amazed and delighted at what you will be able to accomplish in a very short time.

Why your prospects think and process the way they do is not what is important. Which brain language and dialect they speak is what is important.

By now, you are probably starting to understand why you are so successful and comfortable with one kind of prospect over another. Just like the exercises to teach you how to speak the different brain languages, I will now teach you how to speak both dialects. Mastering both the three languages and the two dialects will allow you to communicate with the six combinations that exist all around you. This will move you closer and closer to the top of that 25% to 1000% sales increase I told you about. You can do the math for yourself based on your own compensation plan to determine the economic value to you.

Here are the profiles for both the patriarchal and matriarchal dialects to help you determine which dialect you speak. Remember that these are not absolutes. Just like the three different brain languages, we all have both of these characteristics, qualities and dialects within us. Review and compare both sets of qualities, and determine which one you are the **most** like.

PATRIARCHAL PROFILE

- You prefer to be alone or with one or two select friends.
- At social events you gravitate towards someone you already know instead of mixing with the group.
- You have more male friends than female friends.
- When you have deep meaningful conversations, it is normally with someone you know really well.
- You view relationships and business from your position rather than the position of your entire team.

- The person you aspired to be like as a child was a dominant person.
- When forced to make difficult decisions that affect other people you are able to detach yourself from your emotions and act decisively.
- You need time to be by yourself and you become uncomfortable if you do not have time alone.
- You view most decisions as affecting you personally.
- You see yourself as, or have been told you are a loner.

MATRIARCHAL PROFILE

- You prefer to be with people rather than alone.
- At social events you find it fairly easy to mix with the group.
- You have more female friends than male friends.
- When you have deep meaningful conversations it can be with someone you just met.
- You view relationships and business from the team or group point of view.
- The person you aspired to be like as a child was a team player or non-dominant type of person.
- When forced to make difficult decisions that affect other people, it is difficult for you to detach yourself from your emotions. You may be able to terminate someone but it bothers you.
- You may enjoy time by yourself, however you prefer to be with people, friends, and family. You get "edgy" if you are alone too long.
- You view most decisions as affecting the group, family, or team.
- You see yourself as, or have been told that you mix well with people.

Again, don't judge this process. The answers are only important to help you understand yourself better and to learn how to understand, communicate, and work better with others. If you agreed with all of one of the groups, you are a "Classic," and as a result you will find it more difficult to learn to float between dialects. Remember, we all enjoy and want to do business with people that are the most like us.

One of the most important steps of your opening interview is to start with some recall questions so you can determine which brain language and dialect your prospect speaks. As you are getting to know your prospect, ask some of the following or similar questions.

- How long have you been (job title)?
- What position did you hold before this one?
- Who was the most influential person in your professional success, do you recall?
- Do you have a degree in business or are you a self-made business success?
- What is the name of the teacher or professor who had the most impact on you when you were in school, do you recall?
- Who is the person you most admire in business?
- Tell me more about …(fill in the blank).
- What is the most important quality in business to you?
- Where were you born?
- What do you like best about …(fill in the blank).

As they speak, notice their eye movements and the brain language dialogue words they use. Again, let me review the three different brain language eye movements and dialogue and dialect words. The following explanations assume a right-handed person. Remember that the movements will be reversed for a left-handed person. If their eyes move up and to the left to recall and they use visual words like, "**See, saw, seen, picture, vision, view,**" they are Visual thinkers. Once you have determined his or her brain language, listen closely for dialect words. If they use words like "**Team, us, we, our,**" they are Visual-Matriarch or V-M. If they use words like, "**Me, my, I, I'll,**" they are a Visual-Patriarch or V-P.

If your subject's eyes move left towards the left ear and they use auditory words like, "**Hear, heard, listen, said, say,**" they are Auditory thinkers. If you hear dialect words like "**Team, us, we, our,**" they are an Auditory-Matriarch or A-M. Just like the visual example, if they use words like, "**Me, my, I, I'll,**" they are Auditory-Patriarch or A-P.

If the person you are observing looks down and to the left to recall and uses words like, "**Feel, felt, follow, been, is, was, touch, experience,**" he or she is a Kinesthetic thinker. If you hear dialect words like "**Team,**

us, we, our," they are Kinesthetic-Matriarch or K-M. Again, just like the auditory and visual examples, if they use words like, "**Me, my, I,** or **I'll,**" they are Kinesthetic-Patriarch or K-P.

The following chart may help you understand the different brain language and dialect combinations.

There are six brain language and dialect combinations; their two-letter codes are:

Visual – Matriarch = V-M
Visual – Patriarch = V-P
Auditory – Matriarch = A-M
Auditory – Patriarch = A-P
Kinesthetic – Matriarch = K-M
Kinesthetic – Patriarch = K-P

You already speak one brain language and dialect fluently. As soon as you recognize the other brain languages and dialects, speaking them becomes fun and easy. If someone is a V-P and you are a V-M, notice how easy it is to feed back his or her dialogue in the first person. It is not difficult for you to talk about him or her and position what you are selling as, "benefiting him or her personally." You will notice that they will refer to themselves with words like "Me, my, and my point of view." It is simple, easy, and fun to say, "You, your, and your point of view." You will see for yourself that they will respond very favorable to you.

The secret that will permanently move the decimal point to the right on your paycheck and keep it there is PDR. Don't fall victim to using this **success system** occasionally or returning to your old ways of selling. The more you work with this **success system** the better you will get at it. Use it all of the time and you will master it. When you watch TV, notice what brain language people being interviewed are speaking. Notice what brain language and dialect your favorite actor or athlete is speaking.

Several of the most successful athletes are Kinesthetic-Matriarchs. Watch as they are interviewed on TV. Notice if their eyes move down and to the left to recall and down and to the right when they think or construct thoughts. Notice if they appear as gentle and caring people that talk about the "team" or the "experience." You will notice that the

Matriarchs are easier to like than the Patriarchs because they don't talk about themselves very often. Patriarchs use words like "I, me, and my." Matriarchs say, "we, us, and our." True Matriarchs only talk about themselves when they are pressed for an answer that pertains to their performance or they need to reference something they said or did personally. Even then, they appear almost embarrassed to talk about themselves.

Co-dialectal people can move back and forth from Patriarchal to Matriarchal as needed. They are almost as rare as the fully-integrated, trilingual brain language thinkers are. The fully-integrated, trilingual brain language thinker and the co-dialectal person are proof positive that becoming a co-dialectal, trilingual person is possible for all of us. These abilities can be learned and applied. Here is another Steven Lloyd-ism.

> *"What one person can master, you can master, too!"*

To become co-dialectal, use the same process you used to increase your brain language ability to become trilingual. Spend an entire day thinking and speaking in the opposite dialect. You will notice a big difference in just one day. If you are a Patriarch, pretend that you are talking to a young and very sensitive child for the entire day. Speak in "we, our, us" dialogue. You will notice that your ability to relate to the opposite dialect will increase dramatically in just one day. You will hear things like, "You are so kind and understanding today!" If you are a Matriarch, pretend that you are in an important business deal for the entire day, and you need to know all of the results and how they will affect you. Pretend that you only have one day to learn all of the "bottom line" answers. You will hear things like, "You sure seem different today." Both of these feedback responses are proof that your dialect PDR is working!

The goal is to get you to understand yourself and how you perceive the world around you. Becoming aware of the other dialect will help you develop the other side of your brain. You will become twice as effective and you will enjoy your life more. No one likes the feeling of not fitting in. Imagine how it will feel to be able to open and maintain a conversation in one or more languages and dialects. See yourself moving from one language and dialect to another in the same conversation or presentation.

Doesn't that sound great? Well, you are only a few short days from being able to do just that!

Just as you did with the three different brain languages, find two people who represent both dialects. Deliver your presentation to both of the opposite dialects, one at a time. Use both his or her brain language **and** his or her dialect. After you have practiced with one dialect at a time, put both people at the same presentation table and PDR again. Go back and forth between the two different dialects asking both brain language and dialect questions in their language and dialect. It might sound something like this:

"Bob (A-P), does this **sound** like the **bottom line** kind of results you want?" Bob (A-P) answers, "Yes, it **sounds** good to **me**."

"Jane (K-M), how do you **feel** about what I have shared with you? Do you **feel** this will give your **team** the kind of **experience** they want and need?" Jane (K-M) answers, "I'm **following** you just fine and this will definitely **be** good for the **team**!"

"John (V-M), does this **look** like it will work for **everyone** you are concerned about?" John (V-M) answers, "It **looks** great. From my **view**, I think it will work for **everyone**!"

"Helen (A-P), How does this **sound** to **you**, based on what **you told** me **you** wanted?" Helen (A-P) answers, "**Sounds** good to **me**!"

The two *golden keys* that unlock this **success system** are:

- Address a Patriarch with "them-focused" dialogue in his or her brain language. The Patriarch sees, hears, or feels that they are personally responsible for the entire result and that all decisions affect them personally.
- Address a Matriarch with team, or group-focused dialogue in his or her brain language. The Matriarch sees, hears, or feels that they are part of a group. They also BELIEVE that their decisions affect the entire group.

If you will use the same three, 21-day learning and integration system I have already taught you, you will see, hear, and experience for yourself that this **success system** will start and continue to produce dividends beyond your wildest expectations as long as you continue to use it.

As you work at learning this **success system**, you will get better and better results. You will soon learn that you can discover what brain language and dialect combination someone is speaking by just listening to them. It won't be long and you will be able to do this on the telephone. A good exercise is to close your eyes and listen to someone being interviewed on television. Remember that if they are reading a teleprompter they are not expressing **their** natural brain language and dialect. They must be speaking candidly. Watch *Larry King Live*. Close your eyes and listen carefully to the words that they use when they respond to Mr. King's questions.

The next time you are talking to someone on the telephone, ask him or her some recall questions and listen carefully to their responses. Then try speaking in his or her dominant brain language and dialect. Remembering to be aware of this each time you have a conversation with anyone will be a big part of your success in using this **success system**. Before you get into the main reason for your call, make a note to yourself using the two-letter code on page 214 so you know their brain language and dialect.

Just like the formal structure of a formal sales presentation, I have saved sales closing for last. You have one more chapter to go before you graduate and start to experience the results of working in the arena of the World-Class salesperson. Keep reading and you will be amazed and delighted at how simple, easy, and fun closing the sale really is when you work at **Getting Hired Vs Closing the Sale!**

CHAPTER TWELVE
GETTING HIRED Vs CLOSING THE SALE

CLOSING THE SALE HAS NEVER BEEN EASIER!

This is the final **success system**, at least for this book. In chapter four I shared some dialogue with you about using a 15-minute timer when you start your sales presentation. This technique is very effective because it is unique. To my knowledge, only my students are using it. Second, it helps to remove the prospect's fear that you will take up an hour or more of their time. Many salespeople say that they will take only 15 minutes. Then, after an hour or more the salesperson is still, "in there pitching." Many business people have told me that they have on more than one occasion had to ask the salesperson to leave. You can get one of these electronic timers at any Radio Shack store. They are inexpensive and work very well. I use the twin timer so that I have two timers and a clock to use.

In addition to getting your electronic timer, you will also need to prepare your Career Resume Book for your Getting Hired presentation. I have prepared a Career Resume Book in a template format for you so all you have to do is drop in the required custom pieces. (If you want to learn more, see the Resources Section in the back of this book.) The following is a format for preparing your own Career Resume Book from scratch:

- Buy a 1 inch three-ring binder with the slip-in clear plastic on the outside front cover.
- Prepare a color graphic showing your company logo or a promotion piece for the front cover. It should have your company name and your own name on it.
- The first page in your three-ring binder should be printed to say, "My Professional Career Resume Book" in large print taking up the first three lines. Then a current color picture of you.
- The next page (left side) should be a statement page declaring what you do and what you offer.
- The opposite page (right side) can have sample brochures.
- The next page, (left side) is a declaration page stating what your services will do to improve your prospect's business.
- The next page (right side) should show samples of stages or completed projects you have done. If you are new, your manager can help you obtain samples from other reps, and they should be credited as such.
- The following two pages (left and right) should show the progress of the past projects. Imagine looking at before-and-after pictures of a landscaping company.
- If you have several products and or services, use the next two or three sections to repeat this process. This is helpful because you can turn to the exact sample project that applies to each prospect.
- The next section is designed for significant social evidence. This is where you would put in clippings of ads, articles, and testimonial letters from satisfied clients.
- The next section is for review. This is where you "plug in" what you have learned in your fact-finding homework with your prospect. This allows you to use their unique issue and review what you can do to solve it.
- The back section should contain more testimonials from satisfied clients. This is where you provide overwhelming proof that you are the right person for the job.

Think of your Career Resume Book as a greatly expanded pictorial resume. Think of your sales call as a job interview. I will teach you how and when to use your Career Resume Book later in this chapter.

You need to remember the promise you made when you set the appointment. If you used the dialogue for setting appointments from Chapter Four, you made the following promise: "When my presentation starts, I will start a 15-minute timer and when it 'beeps', if there's nothing else you would like to know, I promise to leave as a friend and not take up any more of your valuable time. What is the most open time in your schedule to meet me for 15 minutes, mornings or afternoons?"

It is critical that you not exceed the 15 minutes in the presentation part of your meeting without being invited to do so. Remember, however, you said, "When my presentation starts, I will start a 15-minute timer." This does **not** include the time it takes to meet them and get positioned to make your presentation. The meeting and greeting portion of your appointment should not take more than an additional five to seven minutes. The warm-up or "icebreaking" segment will take an additional five to seven minutes. I have provided you specific dialogue to cover this promise. I have personally field-tested this **success system**, as have hundreds of salespeople I have personally trained. If you follow the **success system** and dialogue as I outline it for you, your sales performance will equal the success I have witnessed and experienced. Remember, no one expects the "meter to be running" the minute you walk in the door! You do, however, have to keep your promise, and I will show you how.

During your initial meeting there are three separate stages. Stage one is the visual acknowledgement. This is when you and your prospect first see each other. This is the reason you should always dress to impress. Dressing to impress does **not** mean that you wear the best clothes you own. I BELIEVE in and teach "one notch above" dressing. This means that if you call on a blue-collar market where your prospects wear work clothes, you should wear casual dress clothes. If you wear your "Sunday best" to call on a blue-collar market, you will be over-dressed. You will make your prospect feel uncomfortable working with you. Conversely, if you call on an executive type of business prospect, even though most major executive firms have relaxed their dress code, you would still want to dress "one notch above" your prospect. In this case, a business suit would be recommended. Always wear dry-clean only clothes when calling on the executive class prospects. You will soon get a grasp for the kind of dress and style that makes you and your prospect feel comfortable, and creates the best impression. Just remember that "one notch above" dressing gives you a distinct advantage.

The second stage is the verbal greeting. The person you are calling on will either come out to greet you or you will be sent or taken back to meet them. It is important that the first phrase out of your mouth be rehearsed so that you introduce yourself correctly and make the best possible impression. I prefer to allow the prospect to start the conversation by using my body language. I smile and nod my head as I slowly move toward the prospect. Because they are expecting you, they will normally respond with something like, "Hi, you must be Steven Lloyd?" If they do this, I respond back with, "Yes I am and you must be Peter Prospect?" By adding a question to my voice, it mentally puts the conversation ball back in their court requiring them to respond. If the prospect does not respond to this technique, I allow them all of the time up to the distance of a handshake between our bodies. Then, I extend my hand, smile and say, "Hi, I'm Steven Lloyd!" This will always elicit a response back from them with their name. Never assume that the person coming to greet you is your prospect. Always ask.

The third stage is the physical contact with the prospect. You may be nervous or uncomfortable when you first meet someone. The handshake is one of the most misunderstood steps to a successful business launching. It may be helpful for you to know the history of the handshake and why it is still employed in business today. Have you ever wondered why we shake hands with the right hand and not the left? In the Roman days of old, most warriors were right-handed. When two soldiers met on the road they would extend their right or sword hand toward the other warrior. This demonstrated that he could not grab his sword and attack. As the other soldier approached on the narrow road he would grab the approaching soldier on the forearm well above the wrist and the other man would also grab him on his forearm. They would hold each other's sword arm as they rotated past each other and went on their way. Over the decades the forearm embrace continued as a form of greeting. It moved farther and farther down the arm until it became a handshake.

Today, the handshake remains as a form of greeting, but it also serves as a form of communication with the other person. If you extend your hand timidly with your body turned sideways to the prospect, your body language sends a negative message. You are perceived as timid or that you are holding back or have something to hide. Timidity is perceived as fear. A perception of fear will always work against you. If, however, you turn your body to fully face your prospect, extend your hand with the palm up in friendship, and embrace their hand firmly, it sends a message of trust and confidence.

Extending your hand palm up and then touching the back of the hand of your prospect with your other hand can also enhance the handshake. This shows openness and helps you connect deeper at the point of greeting. The palm up technique removes subconscious fear from one's childhood. Many of us were slapped on the head. The palm of the other person doing the slapping was always palm down.

Most business people have had enough experience transitioning between the formal greeting into the meeting. You will on occasion need to take the lead. If you find yourself standing in the hallway for more than two minutes or so, try saying something like, "I promised you that I would not take up too much of your time, may we move to your office or conference room?" This will almost always take care of your presentation repositioning.

The next issue you need to deal with is what to do if you are offered something to drink. It is common for a prospect to say, "Would you like a cup of coffee?" Always ask, "Are you going to have a cup?" If they say, "Yes" and you drink coffee, accept their offer. If they say, "Yes" and you don't drink coffee say, "I have had more than my share today but I would really enjoy a glass or cup of water!" Never tell a coffee drinker that you don't drink coffee because you may make them feel that you think people that drink coffee are somehow less than good people. If they say "No" say, "I'm fine too, thank you for offering." Coffee drinkers normally offer coffee all day long. A non-coffee drinker will most often offer coffee or something else to drink. The keys to remember here are:

- Appear to be as much like the prospect as you can without self-compromise.
- Do not complicate your presentation by drinking something that your prospect is not drinking like coffee or soft drinks.

Now that you are in your prospect's office or meeting area, you are now moving into the "icebreaking" or "getting to know them" phase of the professional presentation. Make a mental note of his or her brain language and dialect. Speak to them in their language using their dialect. You will feel a natural sense of rapport build to a level that feels like you have known them for a long time. BELIEVE me, they will feel it too.

The paying of a sincere compliment can enhance rapport. There are some rules to paying compliments that almost always work. One general rule for both genders is, always compliment a possession or achievement. On the first meeting, never compliment without knowing some facts. First, make sure you are in their office. You can say something like, "Have you had this office from the beginning with this firm?" Next, say, "This seems nice, do you like it here?" Next, look around the room and see what they are the most proud of that is visible from your side of the desk. Always phrase your question to find out if what you are looking at is theirs. I once complimented a man's sailfish. I soon learned that it was not his sailfish and that he hated it. It belonged to his boss who made him store it in his office. Now, I say something neutral like, "That is an interesting piece, did you catch it?" Never assume!

As you sit "visiting," look around the room for the best place to transition into your 15-minute presentation. If there is a separate table in the room, that is perfect because it moves him or her from behind their desk. If you have only a one-desk size office to work with, you will need to reposition yourself to a corner of his or her desk. The goal is to change your current physical position and to get physically closer to the prospect with the least amount of barriers between the two of you.

Discovering Your Prospect's
EMOTIONAL BUYING MOTIVATION

Discovering your prospect's EBM (Emotional Buying Motivation) is the single greatest objective in your sales interview. Much like discovering a BELIEF, when you do uncover your prospect's EBM, you will feel energy from your prospect. You will also hear excitement in their voice and see a change in their physical demeanor. The EBM can be either positive or negative. In other words, his or her Emotional Buying Motivation can be either something they want to have, do, or become, or something they want to avoid. If they are coming from a place of desire, their energy will be positive and empowering. If they are coming from fear, they will demonstrate the opposite energy and behavior.

The *golden key* to unlocking the EBM door is a **sincerity of purpose** on your part to truly be an asset to your prospect. The discovery of their EBM will come from a series of questions.

Imagine that you are in your prospect's office. You have done a good job of building rapport. You like them and enjoy their company and you BELIEVE they like and enjoy you, too. The *golden key* phrase that unlocks their permission door that I want you to remember now is, "**I'm just curious.**" I call this a license phrase. It works like magic because it gives the other person's brain a reason for your question. It gives you a "license" to ask what may appear to be a personal question.

In chapter five I explained the two Guards, the Warrior of Intellect and the Adviser of Emotion. Remember, your prospect's Emotional Adviser must feel that you are sincere or it will send a signal to your prospect to "stay guarded" where you are concerned. Your pre-discovery statement should go something like this; "Jane, my hope is that you will allow me to help you achieve whatever goal is really important to you regardless of what I do for a living. **I'm just curious**, what is the number-one goal you are trying to accomplish with your career, and why?" Look at your prospect with an expectant stare as if you expect to learn something really profound and important.

Do not be surprised if he or she becomes a little uncomfortable or even becomes a little more guarded. They are not used to people taking a personal interest in their wants and needs. Most often their time is invested in screening vendors. This is why this technique works so well, if you will just work with it. Any discomfort you may observe comes from the fact that they are considering answering your question. They are listening to their inner Advisers. Do not interrupt their analysis. Allow them to process your question and to respond.

If you get an answer that sounds like it came off of a greeting card and has no passion or energy behind it, that is not their EBM! Just look at your prospect and say, "Interesting, I'm curious, why is that important to you personally?" Again, look at them as if you expect them to say something really profound. Don't be at all concerned about losing rapport or upsetting your prospect. They may ask you why you want to know. Here is the best answer and best professional BELIEF that I have found to date, to be given passage into the Heart of the prospect by the

Adviser of Emotion. Before you proceed, I caution you not to use this tool if you do not really BELIEVE it. Here it is: "The reason I asked you this question is so that I know what you really want to accomplish with your life and career, so that I can help you reach that goal any way I can! I want to be your friend and ally. It doesn't matter to me what you want, I just would like to know that everything I am doing with you is helping you get closer to something that is really important to you!" If you are the kind of person that truly understands that your personal, professional, and economic rewards are a harvest that comes from the seeds of help and support you sow for others to reach their goals and dreams, this will be easy for you.

Once your prospect trusts you intellectually **and** emotionally, they will open up to you. You may be surprised at what you hear. You must control your visual, auditory, and emotional response to whatever they tell you. Normally your prospect's EBM is not some deep dark secret but it may be something they want or need to guard. It may be a secret that they do not want anyone else in the company to know about, like—they may want their boss' job. They may want to leave the company and start their own. If you are not a direct employee of the same company, your prospect IS your "boss" and should be given the same kinds of confidentiality and loyalty as your real employer (at least as far as this sale and account are concerned).

If you feel or sense your prospect "dancing" around your question, repeat your objective like this, "Jane, I really don't care what your personal or professional goals are. I just want you to trust me enough to tell me what you really want so I can help you achieve it. What do you really want?" Again, look at them as if you expect something from them that is profound!

You may be worrying that they might get upset with you. Nothing could be farther from the truth. Unless he or she is a very private and guarded person, they will be delighted that someone cares enough about them to want to know what they want. Ask yourself how you would feel and respond if you and I were to sit down and then I asked you, "What is the most important thing you want to accomplish and how can I help you get it?" Don't you feel cared about? Doesn't that make you feel good and increase the rapport you feel with me even more? Sure it does! As long as the person doing the asking is sincerely trying to help you, we all like attention to our wants and needs.

When your prospect expresses his or her real EBM, you will know it. It has passion and energy within it. Be very careful to respond appropriately and respectfully and not to react to it in a way that will cause them to shut down. Once you have completely won their trust, you may be surprised what they reveal to you. It may be and often does not have anything to do with business or with what they do for a living or even with the reason you are there to see them.

When he or she reveals their Emotional Buying Motive, say something like, "Interesting, why is that important to you?" The why is the most important part of the EBM puzzle that you are trying to piece together. Once you have uncovered what you BELIEVE to be their true Emotional Buying Motive try saying something like this, "Jane, regardless of what I do for a living or if we ever do business together, what can I do to help you?" BELIEVE me, this is so powerful, you will be amazed and delighted how your professional relationship moves into the next Dynamic Dimension.

Your prospect may very well say something like, "You can help me right now by being the best (whatever you do or sell) that you can be." If they do not bring the meeting back around to you, wait until you feel and observe that they have processed whatever emotion they are experiencing. When you are convinced that you are not interrupting a special moment for them, just look at your watch and say, "How are we doing for time, do you need for me to reschedule?" In the 12 years I have worked with the Emotional Buying Motive selling approach, I have always had the prospect come back with something like, "Oh no, please, go ahead with your presentation!" It is human nature for them to feel an equal and compensating value to you based on their perception of what you have just done for them. You can bank on the fact that no one else has made this kind of contribution or even the attempt to find out what your prospect really wants to achieve with his or her life and career.

If you can grasp the concept that you are a resource and not a salesperson, you will automatically ascend into the next Dynamic Dimension of personal and professional growth and development. You will also automatically start receiving the commensurate income and benefits that come from this new level of giving and being. There is no way to avoid it; this is how the universal law of compensation works!

Once you have achieved what I am describing, you will gradually start to experience your sales call interviews in a whole new way. They will take you on a whole new and exciting result. You will be building relationships with your customers, not just trying to sell them something so that you can make a living. This technique will take you way past making a living and well into designing a life which includes wealth and happiness.

Because this is such an important and sensitive part of *Heart Selling*, it is important that you PDR with non-prospects until you become comfortable with this technique. Use this technique with friends, family, and business associates. You will notice that discovering anyone's EBM is easier and faster the better you know them and the more they already trust you. You will also observe and experience a significant increase in the emotional connection in your relationship with your practice partner, similar to what I have described happening with your prospects. Always do your PDR with your EBM (Emotional Buying Motivation) discoveries, one-on-one, and in private.

After you are invited to move into your formal presentation, simply keep your prospect's EBM in your mind and Heart. You will not need to and should **not** reference it directly unless it directly relates to what you are selling. By just keeping the prospect's EBM in mind, it will reflect itself in your presentation. Regardless of what you sell, the prospect can and will see that buying from you will move them closer to having, doing, or being what they really want because they get you in the package of whatever you sell. I call it the *Jockey and Horse* sale. You are the jockey and your product or service is the horse. They might not even want another "horse," however, they can always use another great jockey!

REPOSITIONING TO THE FORMAL PRESENTATION

After you feel a real sense of rapport and you see that your prospect is open to receive your presentation, you need to lead him or her gently to the formal presentation. By now you should be on a first name basis with your prospect. Because I want you to have sample dialogue to use, I will give you an example using my own career and business. You can then "plug in" the words that fit with what you do. The dialogue would go something like this;

"Jane, let me explain why I came to see you today. I want to interview for the job of your sales education and motivation training coach. My reason for being here is **not** to try to sell you anything today but to get hired as the person you will rely on to bring you and your firm the latest "state of the training industry" information, ideas, and sales performance results. I want to be your personal and professional ally and secret weapon. If you hire me, my job is to continue to make you look good to your boss by helping you increase your weekly, monthly, quarterly, and annual sales performance results. This in turn makes your boss look good to his or her boss by showing higher profit numbers. From a professional point of view, that is ultimately what you want, isn't it?" (I have never gotten a "No"!)

"Jane, unlike other people that you may interview, I am not seeking a salary from you. All I will ever ask you for is the opportunity to help you solve the ongoing challenge of increasing your sales numbers year after year. I will work with you to accommodate your current budget or to help you create a training budget. As our joint work produces results, I will show you how other Executive Sales Officers I have worked for were able to successfully increase their sales training budgets. As we successfully increase sales and therefore profits, you can afford to continue to grow and develop your sales and management force. Ultimately, that is how I will win. Does that seem like a workable general concept?"

Normally, his or her mind is now open to see, hear, or experience more. This is where you move to a different physical position and start your presentation and timer and use your Career Resume Book.

To reposition yourself you might say something like this, "Jane, could I have the courtesy of the use of that table so I can show you a few things?" Or, "Jane, can I have the courtesy of using the corner of your desk so I can show you a few things?" Most people will bend over backwards to keep from being discourteous. As you ask the question, start to physically move your body toward the spot you want. They will almost always accommodate you.

I will use the sample dialogue that I would use for interviewing for the job of their sales education and motivation training coach. Fill in your own unique product or service dialogue into this model.

After you have repositioned yourself, it is time to keep your 15-minute promise. Take out your timer that has been preset to 15 minutes and face it towards you. Take out your Career Resume Book or whatever type of presentation materials you prefer to use. Then say, "I promised you that I would only take 15 minutes to present to you what I BELIEVE I can do to help you personally achieve your professional (whatever you sell) goals for this firm." Start the timer and your presentation. You should be able to tell your sales story in 15 minutes. You need to PDR so you know what 15 minutes looks, sounds, and feels like. Every now and then, as you present, look at the timer that is facing you. Remember the promise was that you would leave after a 15-minute presentation **unless** they invited you to stay! Regardless of where you are in your presentation, when the timer says, "14:50" you say these words, "Jane, regardless of all of the important things we have talked about today, the most important thing I could share with you to insure your personal success in your current position is, 'BEEP, BEEP, BEEP." Turn the timer off and stop talking. Don't say another word. Wait for your prospect to say something like, "And, so, yes, well, what is it?" BELIEVE me, they will say it! You say, "Can I take that question as your invitation for me to stay past our agreed presentation time?" Unless you have taken up too much time in the first steps of your interview process, they will almost always invite you to stay longer. They will also be very impressed with your use of this technique. My students report that they have had World-Class results using this **success system**. Now, the answer to her question is, "I am your personal and professional ally and secret weapon. You, Jane, get all of the credit for the work I do. All that you have to figure out is, how you are going to pay my fees!"

This is a good time to test the "buying temperature" of your prospect. Remember to ask your test question in his or her language and dialect. It would go something like this, "Jane, how does this idea (sound, look, or feel) to you?" If Jane is a Matriarch you would add, "Does this concept (sound, look, or feel) like it will enhance the entire team's position?" If she is a Patriarch you might say, "Jane, does this concept (sound, look, or feel) like it will enhance your position by enhancing your bottom line results?"

The intensity of the energy she responds with tells you if she is ready to say "Yes" to your getting hired question. If you BELIEVE she is ready, you could ask, "So when do you want me to start?" If she was not ready, you could miss the opportunity completely. I prefer the self-closing technique like, "Jane, how are you required to report your sales performance results?" Regardless of what she says, ask, "When do you do your budget?" Regardless of what she says, ask, "How much did you budget for sales training or sales promotion (or whatever you do or sell)?" Next say, "If you and I were to take the needed steps to turn your results in the direction you need them to go or to maximize your sales potential, when would you want to have your first meeting?"

The strategy is to ask value-based questions that eliminate their waiting time. If you sell real estate, in a listing, *Getting Hired* presentation you might ask, "When do you want or need to be settled in your new home in your new city?" Simply add that date to the average, "listing to sale average," for your market. Then say, "Given the timetable for a well-positioned and -priced listing in this market and the timetable average for your purchase and the 'settling in' to your new home timetable, it would appear that we should have had your property on the market last week! We can catch up if we start now, and you are willing to do what we need to do to get your property ready for the market. Are you willing?"

The same strategy works for any product or service. In my business, even though there are a lot of good speakers and trainers, there is only one of me. When my calendar is booked and retained, that time is taken. You can use the fact that you have to work with manufacturing, delivery, support staff, or marketing time limitations. In planning, here is another Steven Lloyd-ism for you.

> "*Double the time and money estimates on every project and you will be amazed how often you are right!*"

In other words, don't be afraid that you are misleading your prospect about how long it is going to take to deliver exactly what he or she wants and needs to get the agreement today. It almost always takes longer than you think it will anyway! Helping your prospect start early is always an advantage to him or her. No one ever complains that you have helped them accomplish their wants or needs too soon!

Like all good things, this too must end to make way for the next dynamic experience. There is a new and exciting life and career just waiting for you to claim. Please let me hear from you and how you are doing. One of these days you and I will meet in person. I look forward to hearing what wonderful things you have done with your life and career. Thank you for allowing me to be your guide on this part of your life's journey.

I would like to leave you with one last thought. Work as if you will live forever, live as if you will die tomorrow, dance like no one is watching, love like you have never been hurt, and always, *Sell From The Heart!*

THE BEGINNING!

ABOUT THE AUTHOR

Steven Lloyd entered professional selling at the age of nineteen. Many called him a natural. He claims that he was just "green" enough to really listen to his sales manager and do exactly what he was taught to do. The president of the first insurance company he worked for, Federal Life and Causality, called to congratulate him on breaking a company record his first week in the insurance business.

Steven Lloyd kept breaking record after record in several industries. He took the worldwide # 1% spot with the ITT Hartford Insurance Group two years in a row. He also helped build and manage the largest rural marketing insurance agency in the USA. As the youngest real estate broker and homebuilder in the United States, Mr. Lloyd developed one of the largest real estate companies in northern Wisconsin.

Mr. Lloyd served with distinction as the Western Regional Vice President of the Realtors National Marketing Institute. Recognized for his excellence, he was selected by Dave Stone to serve as the Vice President of the Stone Institute of Real Estate Marketing and Management. Mr. Stone acted as Mr. Lloyd's personal mentor, investing two years, teaching him the finer points of speaking, training, and consulting.

Having a love for higher education and a desire to help our future leaders, Steven Lloyd founded a college and career-planning firm. Within four years, using many of the **success systems** outlined in this book, this firm became the largest college and career-planning firm in the world, serving nearly 50,000 clients in three countries.

Steven Lloyd is an active member of both the National Speakers Association and the North Texas Speakers Association.

From small start-up companies to the largest firms in the world, Mr. Lloyd works with a wide range of organizations including:

Rockwell International
ITT Hartford Insurance
Disney Financial Group
The Sales Marketing Counsel
The National Realtors Association

Zurich U.S.
Lennar Homes
WMA Securities
Coldwell Banker
Allstate Insurance
Munters of America
Best Exterior Design
ProStar ADT Security
CSI Employer Services
Wood Brothers Homes
Reliable Life Insurance
Century-21 Real Estate
Wisconsin National Life
Con-Way Transportation Service
The National Life Underwriter's Association
Trade Associations in many other fields, worldwide

Steven Lloyd is now the recognized leader in the field of Emotional Selling. He is available for keynote speeches, seminars, and workshops. He teaches the Sales Mastery Course, Selling From The Heart, Effortless Motivation, Success From The Heart, Managing From The Heart, It's About Time–Management, Leadership, and several other World-Class seminars and workshops worldwide.

Steven Lloyd resides in Arlington, Texas.

INDEX

RESOURCES SECTION

Contact information:

Mail: Steven Lloyd Associates   **Telephone:** 817-572-9675
4121 Cross Bend Drive   **Toll Free:** 800-743-9595
First Floor   **Fax:** 208-247-8609
Arlington, TX 76016   **Email:**Mailroom@StevenLloyd.com
Website: www.StevenLloyd.com

The following products and services were created to enhance your personal, professional, and economic lives. All of our products come with a 100% success performance satisfaction guarantee! You can return any of our products, for any reason within 30 days from the date of purchase and 100% of your purchase price will be returned, no questions asked!

ITSN (Image Transfer System Notes) Kit

Everything you need to get started is included with this kit except the stamps! Steven Lloyd will walk you step by step into ITSN success with the included VHS training video. You will be producing Image Transferred notes that cannot be distinguished from handwritten within one hour from the time your kit arrives! In addition, Mr. Lloyd will personally train you on how to use this amazing success system to build your business. Call to order.

Selling From The Heart Audio Success System

This six-audiocassette and workbook success system expands on the book with the same title. You receive the highest quality recorded training tapes featuring Steven Lloyd. He will walk you through all of the success systems and processes included in his book. This is your chance to own the audio version and the workbook of the number one emotional sales training success system in the world. Call to order.

Chairperson of the Board single Audiocassette

One of the most powerful and positive gifts you will ever give to yourself is complete and total control of your own thoughts! In this amazing success system, Steven Lloyd will walk you through the powerful Chairperson of the Board process. You will see, feel, and experience your self-confidence expand with just one listening. Each time you listen, you will experience greater and greater personal confidence and self-control. You will become the Chairperson of the Board of your own brain! Call for more information.

Fresh Sales Leads

Get the sales leads software and 1000 fresh, up-to-date sales leads that you can sort by ZIP code or SIC code. Each sales lead has been telephone verified for accuracy. Software and your first 1000 sales leads, call for current pricing.

RESOURCES SECTION

Selling From The Heart Quantity Book Orders

We have been asked repeatedly for a quantity order discount for the book Selling From The Heart. If you would like to give this book to your staff, offer it as a premium or incentive, or resell the book, the following pricing applies:

11-20	$14.36 each
21-50	$13.95 each
51-100	$11.99 each
101-500	$ 9.99 each
501-1000	$ 7.99 each
1001-2500	$ 6.38 each
2501-5000	$ 5.59 each
5001-10000	$ 4.79 each
10001-25000	$ 3.20 each

25001+ Special pricing with special dedication page available.

Good-Night Sleep Right & Good-Morning, Let's Make It A Great Day!

Using this amazing success system will build your self-esteem, self-image, and personal motivation faster than anything you have ever tried! Based on the years of research on the levels of your mind's receptivity to input, this two audiocassette success system is designed to help you slip off to sleep with beautiful and deeply relaxing music and sounds specially recorded in nature. As you enter the Alpha State, Steven Lloyd's soothing and professionally trained voice will gently and audibly insert the building blocks required for you **to feel great** about you! The Good-Morning counterpart audiocassette will gently wake you from a deep and restful sleep. As you are slowly and gently awakened, Steven Lloyd will gradually increase your brain wave energy and start the Positronic Great Day planning process. Imagine starting and ending your day with one of the most positive success coaches in the world! Call to order.

Seven Minutes Before You Present

Steven Lloyd has learned that listening to just the right stimulation before a sales presentation created a positive difference of as much as 50% in the sales call success! What to listen to and for how long became a multi-year study. If the message is too long, you must stop the tape midstream. Your mind is not focused on the next sale, it is centered on the part of the tape you haven't finished listening to! If the tape is too short, you do not get the full mental integration and stimulation that is needed to take your mind off of what is not working and put it back on what does work. After years of research and testing, Steven Lloyd found the answer and created the success system called, *Seven Minutes Before You Present!* This tool will serve you over and over again, before you present. It is specially designed so the exact same message is reproduced on both sides of the tape so it is automatically cued up and ready to prepare you for your next sales call. Call now to order this twin sided audiocassette.

RESOURCES SECTION

Effortless Motivation

Have you noticed that there are certain things that when you think them or do them that you get the same result? Steven Lloyd has discovered the secrets and now presents them to you in a personal motivation success system that will pull your life forward like a Locomotive! You will learn success secrets as simple as turning on a special kind of light bulb and never feeling blue or down ever again! You will learn secrets that you did not even know existed but that will get you up in the morning singing and ready to take on the day! This success system will become so valuable to you that you will never lend it to anyone! By just listening and following the easy and fun-training, you will feel energy that you didn't know you had. Your life and career will feel like you are being pulled forward by a powerful Locomotive! Steven Lloyd will be your personal Effortless Motivation coach through this Audio Success System.

Sales Mastery

Are you a 21st Century competent sales professional? What standard are you measuring by? Sales Mastery, The Twelve Sales Competencies, will carry you into the next Dynamic Dimension of your professional sales career! This sales mastery program will bring your skills, talents, and professional abilities up to where they need to be in this new millennium! Steven Lloyd will personally walk you through each of the twelve lessons in this Audio Success System. Prepare yourself for a World-Class explosion in your life and career.

MRI-Personal and Professional Profile

Have you ever wondered what you are really good at and what special gifts, talents, and abilities you have and how to apply them? This success system will show you exactly where your strengths and weaknesses are. This personal and professional tool will show you what you are good at and where you need to grow. You will learn how to motivate yourself by learning what really motivates you. You also learn what the specific things are that you need to avoid. You will be amazed and delighted at how accurate this profile is, no more guessing! This tool is required for all of Steven Lloyd's associates so he can personally coach them to success. Call for more information!

BRC PERSONAL COACHING

Based on Mr. Lloyd's calendar availability, he will help you discover what is holding you back from World-Class performance and help you replace that belief with one that will draw your life and career forward automatically!

LIVE STEVEN LLOYD EVENTS

One of the things that sets Steven Lloyd apart from the crowd of speakers and trainers is his amazing ability to get inside an organization and design a custom training program around your needs. Custom training will drive the custom results you want and need. Professional fees for a full day of custom training for your group are available upon request.

The following are Steven Lloyd's most requested topics

Sales Mastery • Selling From The Heart • Effortless Motivation
Managing From The Heart • Success From The Heart
It's About Time–Management • Leadership
Any of these topics can be custom tailored to your organization's unique needs.